MVIEW'99

Proceedings

IEEE Workshop on Multi-View Modeling & Analysis of Visual Scenes (MVIEW'99)

June 26, 1999

Fort Collins, Colorado

Sponsored by

IEEE Computer Society Technical Committee on
Pattern Analysis and Machine Intelligence

IEEE
COMPUTER
SOCIETY

Los Alamitos, California

Washington • Brussels • Tokyo

Copyright and Reprint Permissions: Abstracting is permitted with credit to the source. Libraries may photocopy beyond the limits of US copyright law, for private use of patrons, those articles in this volume that carry a code at the bottom of the first page, provided that the per-copy fee indicated in the code is paid through the Copyright Clearance Center, 222 Rosewood Drive, Danvers, MA 01923.

Other copying, reprint, or republication requests should be addressed to: IEEE Copyrights Manager, IEEE Service Center, 445 Hoes Lane, P.O. Box 133, Piscataway, NJ 08855-1331.

The papers in this book comprise the proceedings of the meeting mentioned on the cover and title page. They reflect the authors' opinions and, in the interests of timely dissemination, are published as presented and without change. Their inclusion in this publication does not necessarily constitute endorsement by the editors, the IEEE Computer Society, or the Institute of Electrical and Electronics Engineers, Inc.

IEEE Computer Society Order Number PRO0110
ISBN 0-7695-0110-9
Library of Congress Catalog Number: 99-62868

Additional copies may be ordered from:

IEEE Computer Society	IEEE Service Center	IEEE Computer Society
Customer Service Center	445 Hoes Lane	Asia/Pacific Office
10662 Los Vaqueros Circle	P.O. Box 1331	Watanabe Bldg., 1-4-2
P.O. Box 3014	Piscataway, NJ 08855-1331	Minami-Aoyama
Los Alamitos, CA 90720-1314	Tel: + 1-732-981-0060	Minato-ku, Tokyo 107-0062
Tel: + 1-714-821-8380	Fax: + 1-732-981-9667	JAPAN
Fax: + 1-714-821-4641	mis.custserv@computer.org	Tel: + 81-3-3408-3118
E-mail: cs.books@computer.org		Fax: + 81-3-3408-3553
		tokyo.ofc@computer.org

Editorial production by Lorretta Palagi

Cover art design and production by Joseph Daigle/Studio Productions

Printed in the United States of America by The Printing House

Table of Contents

IEEE Workshop on Multi-View Modeling & Analysis of Visual Scenes—MVIEW'99

Message from the General Co-Chairs

Welcome to the IEEE Workshop on Multi-View Modeling & Analysis of Visual Scenes! The purpose of this workshop is to bring together researchers interested in the representation and manipulation of static or dynamic 3D scenes from multiple views. In recent years, there has been fast and noticeable progress along the following paths: (1) Image-based rendering techniques have been developed in the computer vision and graphics communities showing the promise of creating photo-realistic simulations of real visual scenes, (2) the area of structure-from-motion has evolved into a body of results related to the representation of 3D space and its camera views in terms of collections of functions representing both the geometric and photometric variability of image space, and (3) advances in multi-view stereo reconstruction have led to impressive results in recovering geometrically and photometrically complex shapes from large collections of images. Taken together, the fast progress along those lines is leading to new ways to formulate the traditional problems of structure-from-motion, motion estimation, reconstruction, and image-synthesis.

In all, 27 papers were submitted to the workshop, of which 10 were selected for presentation. Each paper was reviewed by at least two members of the program committee (including the chairs) and the highest ranked papers are included here. These papers belong to one of four topics: (1) 3D shape recovery, (2) calibration and structure from motion, (3) image-based modeling using photometry, and (4) image-based modeling of dynamic scenes.

Our special thanks go to Steve Shafer, the Chair of the IEEE PAMI Technical Committee, for his support, and Bruce Draper, Ross Beveridge, and Chuck Dyer who, as members of the CVPR organizing committee, helped greatly in making this workshop a reality. Last but not least, we would like to thank all members of our program committee for their encouragement and for reviewing the papers.

General Co-Chairs

Kiriakos Kutulakos
University of Rochester, USA

Amnon Shashua
Hebrew University, Israel

Workshop Committee

General Co-Chairs

Kiriakos Kutulakos
University of Rochester, USA

Amnon Shashua
Hebrew University, Israel

Program Committee

P. Anandan, Microsoft
Michael Cohen, Microsoft
Chuck Dyer, UW–Madison
Olivier Faugeras, INRIA and MIT
Michal Irani, Weizmann Institute
Ramesh Jain, UC–San Diego
Takeo Kanade, CMU
Jitendra Malik, UC–Berkeley
Tomaso Poggio, MIT
Steve Seitz, CMU
Richard Szeliski, Microsoft
Seth Teller, MIT
Demetri Terzopoulos, University of Toronto
Andrew Zisserman, Oxford University

Session I

3D Shape Recovery

The Impact of Dense Range Data on Computer Graphics

Lars Nyland, David McAllister, Voicu Popescu, Chris McCue, Anselmo Lastra,
Paul Rademacher, Manuel Oliveira, Gary Bishop, Gopi Meenakshisundaram, Matt Cutts, and Henry Fuchs
University of North Carolina, Chapel Hill, NC 27599-3175

Abstract

The ability to quickly acquire dense range data of familiar environments has been met with enthusiastic response in our graphics laboratory. In this paper, we describe our prototype range collection system, based on a scanning laser rangefinder and a high-resolution digital color camera, that allows us to create panoramic color photographs where every pixel has an accurate range value. To accommodate occlusions, the data acquisition process is repeated from multiple locations and the results are registered with software. We discuss the acquisition system and review how the data from this prototype system have been used in existing graphics projects. We speculate about future improvements to range acquisition hardware and how those improvements impact graphics applications. The data acquired from our system is just a hint of what will be available in the future and we conclude with speculation about the impact of such data on graphics hardware and algorithms, since prevailing graphics hardware and software do not support this data well.

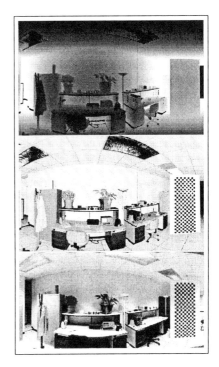

Figure 1. Samples of the range and color data collected from our hardware teaching lab. At the top is a gray-scale range image, below that is the reflected laser intensity image, and at the bottom is a color panorama of the scene. Images such as these are used to create color images with depth.

1. Introduction

Dense range data, where dense means at least one range sample per milliradian, has the potential to change our view of 3D computer graphics. Our particular area of interest has been in enhancing image-based rendering by providing color images of real scenes where each pixel has accurate range information. Thus, in addition to range image acquisition, we have also collected high-resolution color images from the same point-of-view, and built a prototype software system that builds high-resolution color photographs with depth suitable for image warping. An example of the range and color data is shown in figure 1.

The availability of range data collection has also been useful in advancing a variety of other graphics and geometry projects in our lab. For example, the collection of range

data in the "Office of the Future" gives static information about the geometry of projection surfaces for immersive telecollaboration. As range image acquisition systems improve, dynamic range data will allow the collaborators to walk about, viewing the collaboration scene in true 3D.

A well-established research area is building geometric models from range data (point clouds and range images), and we have some new algorithms that quickly consume the range data, simplifying it to only a few percent of its original complexity.

Two additional image-based rendering applications use the dense range data. The first is our *multiple-center-of-*

Please visit http://www.cs.unc.edu/~ibr/pubs/nyland-mview99/ for a full-color version of this paper.

projection images where, potentially, each range sample is taken from a different, but known, location. This allows us to acquire data throughout an environment, substantially reducing occluded areas in a single data set, producing distorted images that are correctly reprojected.

The second is our work on *image-based objects*. Range data of an object is acquired from several locations, the images are then registered and warped to a single point-of-view. This representation has the advantage that occluded areas are drastically reduced while preserving properties of single-image warping, such as occlusion compatible ordering of rendering to preserve proper occlusion.

The final area discussed is the registration (both user-assisted and automatic) of range images taken from different locations in the same environment. One automatic technique improves upon the *iterated-closest-point method* [3] by taking into account the presence of shadows. A separate method for exploring automatic registration looks at 3D Hough transformations of separate range images.

The hardware system we have assembled is a proof-of-concept, and as such, it allows us to speculate about the future impact of high-density range images. Current hardware and algorithms in computer graphics have not considered the existence of high-density range images, and with the growing availability of similar commercial devices, new methods of handling such data need to be considered. For instance, what can be done with 100 million color samples that have positions in three dimensions? Currently, not much more than simplification, but perhaps it is time to think about new trends in rendering hardware, rendering algorithms, model-building and illumination based on high-density color and range data.

This paper describes our prototype range acquisition system, the calibration procedures, the specifics of the data collected, registration of multiple range images, the process of matching range data with color images, and the impact that it has had on our research projects. We conclude with goals for future acquisition systems, citing potential impact on graphics research.

2. Hardware System

Our prototype data collection system consists of a commercial laser rangefinder, a high-resolution digital camera, a panning unit, with a PC to control the devices and collect the color and range data. The components are all mounted on a cart to provide mobility.

Scanning, Laser Rangefinder. Our rangefinder is a commercially available scanning laser rangefinder from Acuity Research [21]. It is a time-of-flight rangefinder that can acquire range data at up to 50K samples/sec. It can accurately determine range from 0 to 15 meters, with better accuracy at closer ranges.

The scanning mirror sweeps the laser beam in a vertical plane with a 60° occlusion (aimed downward). The scanning mirror has a 4096-position shaft encoder to aid in determining where the laser is aimed.

Pan-Tilt Unit. A pan-tilt unit from Directed Perception [17] controls the orientation of the scanning plane. The rangefinder is placed on the pan-tilt unit such that the position where the laser reflects off the scanning mirror is on the panning axis. The panning device has 14,000 steps in 180°; thus, to acquire samples every milliradian, we typically move 3 or 4 steps between each successive scan.

The Color Camera. To collect color data, we use a Canon/Kodak EOS D2000 digital camera. It has high resolution (1728x1152 pixels), accessibility to the raw CCD data, and FireWire communication. The lens in use is the Canon 14mm flat-field lens, chosen to acquire a wide field-of-view, considering that the camera's digital CCD is smaller than 35mm film.

During acquisition, we disable automatic exposure and focus, set the aperture at $f/11$ to get a depth-of-field from 0.5m to ∞, and set the exposure time as necessary to accommodate the aperture for the entire scene. The wide field of view of any panorama typically leads to very large differences in illumination, making a single exposure setting problematic. Currently, we use additional lighting to more evenly illuminate the panorama, but are working on acquiring high dynamic range images, as in [4].

3. Calibration

Since the system is a prototype cobbled together from many parts, calibration procedures were necessary to determine where the laser beam is pointing. These include calibration of the mirror's angle, the scanning motor's position, and the panning device's positioning. The camera also required calibration to determine lens distortion.

Calibrating the Range. The rangefinder is well calibrated by the manufacturer to return accurate measurements over a wide range of values (0 to 15m). Still, there are a few steps a user can take to improve the range values read. First, the rangefinder can return a more confident value if it has a longer period to make a measurement. Knowing this, we typically set the collection rate to 1/2 to 1/3 of the peak rate, and have seen dramatic improvements in the data.

The second is limiting the maximum range value that the rangefinder will return. The rangefinder modulates the laser light to create an interference pattern, so to avoid harmonics, it must look at the longest possible distances first. If this distance is set to be shorter than the maximum, the device can settle on a modulation frequency more quickly, returning a better indication of the range.

Calibrating the Latitudinal Angle. The scanning mirror controls the latitudinal angle (ϕ), and we read its position from the attached 4096-position shaft encoder. Since we are typically taking 5,000–10,000 samples per revolution, it is clear that we must interpolate the shaft position, since subsequent readings may report identical shaft positions.

To do this, we assume constant motor speed over the time required to collect a 1K buffer of samples. It is not possible to know exactly when the encoder moves from one position to the next, but since we have a large number of samples, we can estimate where the transitions occur by performing a least-squares line fit using the points around the transitions.

Calibrating the Longitudinal Angle. Determining the actual angle around the polar axis relies not only upon the panning motor position, but on the angle of the 45° mirror as well. We devised a simple experiment to determine both at the same time.

In a room, we aim the laser horizontally at a wall so it is roughly perpendicular, marking its position. We then move the scanning mirror over the pole 180°, aiming at the opposite wall, and mark that position. We then pan the device 180°, where it should coincide with the first mark. We mark that position, and again move the scanning mirror over the pole to point at the second mark. We mark its position. If all the hardware were perfect, the two marks on each wall would be coincident, but due to errors, they are not. From the separation of the points and knowing the distance from the rangefinder to the points, the panning error and mirror error are both determined. The values we found are 14,039 steps in 180°, and 44.89° (the mirror error also affects the latitude). At a distance of 4m, this moves the data sample more than 3cm.

4. Data Collected

The range data collected consist of quad-tuples of range, longitude and latitude angles (θ and ϕ), and the intensity of the reflected laser light. Two visualizations of the data are shown in figure 1, which are spherical panoramic images (not fisheye) showing the range and reflected laser intensity values at regular latitude-longitude positions. After the data is collected, it can be processed to correct for the calibration values found.

The color data simply consists of a panoramic set of images taken with the camera's nodal point coincident with

that of the rangefinder's (a custom mounting bracket ensures this). The camera is rotated (using the pan-tilt unit) stopping every 24° to acquire a 55° x 77° image.

5. Combining Range and Color Data

After the data is collected, substantial processing is required to combine range data with color information. The result is a color image with accurate range information for every pixel in an image.

Undistorting Color Images. All camera lenses have distortions from the pinhole model they are designed to emulate. Fortunately, lens distortion is well studied, and free software exists to determine parameters that aid in undistorting an image [23]. We acquired several dozen photographs and performed the analysis, using the determined parameters to resample the images into an undistorted form. This is necessary, as the distortion placed some pixels 30 pixels away from their ideal pinhole position.

Range Data Resampling and Cleanup. The data from the rangefinder is not on a regular grid, as there is no control between the scanning motor and the sampling hardware. We project all of the range samples onto a spherical grid, apply some error removal and hole filling heuristics, and then produce a spherical image of the range and intensity values.

If the laser beam spans two disparate surfaces during a sampling period, the resulting range is usually between the two surfaces (though not always). We use a voting scheme on our projection grid that looks at the range of the 8 nearest neighbors. If at least 4 are within some tolerance, the value is deemed to be valid, otherwise it is removed. This has the effect of removing all floating samples.

Since the rangefinder's ability to determine distance depends on the amount of light reflected, we cannot acquire range information for very dark or specular objects. Objects such as glossy (or even semi-glossy) furniture, dark metal, rubber or plastic objects (wall trim, electronic equipment, plastic trim on furniture), or metallic frames and light fixtures all cause problems.

We use a variation of the Splat-Pull-Push algorithm [6] to place the range data on a regular grid and fill in the holes. The algorithm was designed to perform well on sparse data, but also works very well on dense data like that from the laser rangefinder. The splat portion of the algorithm performs most of the work since the samples are about as dense as the image pixels. The pull and push phases interpolate the samples to fill in places that were not scanned well by the laser. We output two images from this process—a range image and an infrared laser intensity image. These images are used to align the color camera images with the range data.

Alignment. The goal of the alignment procedure is to find the orientation of the camera image that best correlates with the rangefinder image. The laser intensity image cannot be directly correlated to the color image (or even the red channel of the color image) because the illumination of the two images is so different that straightforward image correlation gives poor results. The laser image is illuminated directly by the laser and nothing else (ambient light is removed). The laser image has no shadows, the entire scene is equally illuminated, and specularities occur in different places than in the normally lit scene.

Instead, we perform the alignment on the edges in the images. Edge-detection algorithms work well on the data from the laser rangefinder, but tend to show the high frequency noise in the color images. To solve this problem, we apply a variable conductance diffusion operation (VCD) [24] to the color images. Edge detection on the blurred image then finds only the salient edges. The edge pixels are undistorted according to the distortion parameters found in the camera calibration.

Edge detection is performed on both the range and intensity images from the rangefinder. The edges in these images are then blurred by convolving them with a kernel that has wide support, but whose gradient increases near the center of the kernel. This enhances the search by giving nearby solutions a small error value, but not nearly as small as an exact solution.

We only search over the three angles of registration between the spherical range image and planar color image since we know that the two images share the same center-of-projection. The error value is computed as the degree of edgeness from the rangefinder image that corresponds with the edges in the color image. We use a simulated annealing search strategy, which works well when presented with a reasonable starting point.

Having found values for the 3 angles, we return to the original color images, correct for distortion, and determine the proper distance information. To do so, we project the range information onto the planar grid, making a list of range values for each pixel. Resampling range data is problematic, so we perform a clustering algorithm on the range values for each pixel, setting the range as the average of the largest cluster. This method avoids the error of blending samples across multiple surfaces.

Result. The output of this process is a variation of TIFF with one extra layer (disparity, related to inverse depth) and the camera parameters. This is our standard file format for image-based warping reference data [15].

6. Use in Graphics Projects

This section describes how the color and range data is used in current graphics projects in our lab.

Image-Based Rendering by 3D Warping. The primary motivation in producing the data described here is to support our image-based rendering project [1]. Many different aspects of IBR are being studied, such as representation, visibility, reconstruction, multiple views, hardware acceleration, and hybrid CG systems, and all require source images to render.

The registered color and range images lead naturally to an image-warping walk-through application that renders them with as few artifacts as possible. If the images were rendered as triangle meshes, errors would occur at silhouettes such as table edges, doorways, and other spatial discontinuities, where the mesh would be stretched across the spatial discontinuities.

One of the first steps to perform is silhouette edge detection. While many sophisticated methods for performing this exist, it turns out that simple heuristics perform nearly as well and are extremely easy to compute. One method computes the dot product of the viewing ray with the normal vector of the triangles in the mesh. Silhouettes (and badly sampled surfaces) will have values close to 0, and thus the mesh can be broken at these locations.

We have developed a simple application [9] that uses OpenGL and runs on our Onyx2 hardware as well as the custom PixelFlow hardware [5]. The user interface allows the user to move around the environment arbitrarily, using multiple panoramic source inputs. The effect is very real—during demonstrations, many people believe that we have either taken photographs from a significant number of positions or are somehow showing a video. Images from a walk-through sequence with two panoramas are shown in figure 2. The performance is near real-time.

Optimizations have been made to improve rendering performance by using the PixelFlow graphics hardware. For instance, it is possible to perform incremental warping calculations where the warping arithmetic that applies to groups of pixels is performed once and only the pixel-specific arithmetic is performed for each pixel. We have also developed a custom rendering primitive called an image tile. We can cull at the image tile level, providing a dramatic improvement in rendering. The rendering of an image tile is also where the incremental arithmetic is performed.

As a further extension, we have also developed a new point primitive for rendering, which we call the Voronoi-region primitive. It is basically a cone-shaped point rather than a flat disc, aimed at the viewer and falling off in z as its radius increases. When several of these primitives are

Figure 2. Some sample images of a walk-through of our reading room. The input data is composed of panoramas taken from 2 locations and consists of 10 million samples.

Figure 3. For multiple-center-of-projection images, we show the path taken to acquire the data at the top, the acquired data (distorted middle view), and the appropriate reconstruction of the data.

displayed from a planar surface, they implicitly compute the Voronoi regions of the samples. See [9] for full details.

Immersive, 3D Telecollaboration: the Office of the Future. An immersive, telecollaboration project [20] is underway that seeks to share workspaces by projecting images of remote locations onto nearly every surface possible, including irregular and dynamic surfaces. The ceiling of the office is populated with projectors, and cameras are strategically placed in unobtrusive locations for two-way interaction.

Currently, range information provided by the system described here could be used to provide the range of the static structures in the shared environment. This information is used to not only locate all the projection surfaces but to locate the projectors as well, so that the position of each pixel from each projector in the room can be computed.

Multiple-Center-of-Projection Images. MCOP images correctly reconstruct 3D scenes where every pixel in the source image was potentially acquired from a different, but known, position [19]. MCOP images have the advantage that objects can essentially be scanned, but the data is still a single image. If a strip camera is the acquisition model, then pose information is only required for each column of data.

The MCOP project was the first client of the ranging system described here. We attached the UNC Hi-Ball tracking system to the rangefinder, made the acquisition software network-aware, and slowly rolled the range acquisition cart in the tracked environment.

In figure 3, we show a photo of our lab environment with the rangefinder's path superimposed. We then show the resulting image that was collected, colored by hand to distinguish the important parts of the scene. Finally, we show the reconstructed image.

Image-Based Objects. Image-based objects [16] are composed of six layered-depth images [22] of an object properly registered. An IBO can be displayed from an arbitrary viewpoint where it will be rendered correctly. Applications of image-based objects include virtual museums, web-based catalogs and computer games. Multiple IBO's can be composed together and still be properly rendered, since McMillan's results about occlusion compatible ordering [12, 11] for rendering apply to one or more IBO's.

7

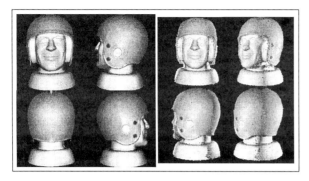

Figure 4. On the left are the 4 input images of a coin-bank. On the right are views of the reconstructed IBO from a variety of viewpoints.

Figure 5. On the left is a texture-mapped rendition of simplified geometry from our reading room data. On the right, we have zoomed in and revealed the mesh structure of the simplified data.

One benefit of image-based objects is that of bandwidth. Sending an IBO to a web-browser is not much more costly than sending an animated GIF, yet with an IBO, the user can move the viewpoint arbitrarily. Additionally, an IBO can be rendered interactively, giving the user instant feedback.

An example of 4 of the images used to build an IBO and their rendering are shown in figure 4. The images only use the laser light, but future objects will also have color.

Reconstruction of Geometry. A fast, memory efficient, linear time algorithm that generates a manifold triangular mesh has been developed [13]. It has been used on standard point cloud data sets as well as the data sets acquired by our prototype range system. The speed of the algorithm is derived from a projection-based approach used to determine the incident faces on a point.

An example of the output from this algorithm is shown in figure 5. The original input has 6.5 million samples, while the result has only ~140k points. The processing time taken to build the mesh was 88 seconds on an Oynx2. The rendering of the reconstructed geometric model is made by applying the intensity image as a texture map onto the created triangle mesh. Despite the drastic reduction in complexity, the model retains the important features of the collected data set.

Registration of Multiple Range Images. We have three methods for registering range image data. One is user-assisted, and was used for all the warped data sets described in this paper. The other two are automatic.

In the user-assisted process, the user selects points from 3 corresponding planes in each data set [10]. The data is shown in a 3D reprojection that can be translated and rotated for easy selection of the points. Once the 3 planes are selected, the fundamental matrix can be found. Error metrics are given, and the process can be repeated as needed.

Other selection techniques have been suggested for plane selection using the 2D display of the range images, including using ordinary box, lasso, and spray paint models. These may be quicker, as it is simple to interact with 2D data displayed on a monitor and manipulated with a mouse.

One automatic method is called the Empty Space Registration Method [18], which is a variant of the Iterated Closest Point Algorithm [3]. In ICP, the data being registered is assumed to be "full," that is, there are no shadows or occlusions and the data is sampled similarly in each data set. In data sets of real environments, there are bound to be occlusions. The empty space registration method considers empty space to the first visible surface and shadow volumes explicitly, knowing that nothing can occupy the empty space and anything can be in the shadows. Results of the search are shown in figure 6, where 2 source views of a computer on a table are shown. The merging shows their almost-correct registration, despite the fact that very little of the scene is shared between the views.

Our second automatic registration method is under development, and is based on a 3D Hough transform of the range data. The edge-detection step is not necessary with the rangefinder data, as the data collected represents the first "edge" in 3D (surface). This method takes each sample and performs the standard Hough transform operation by incrementing all possible buckets of r, θ, and ϕ for each sample. A sample of plane detection is shown in figure 7, where the pixels showing the ceiling of the room have been recovered from the Hough transform of the range data.

7. Additional Applications of Range Data Systems

As-Built Models. Commercial scanners are used to create *as-built models* from range data. One example is an Atlas launch tower was scanned from several locations, all images were inter-registered, and a model was produced for

Figure 6. The top two images show range scans of a workstation. The bottom two images show the automatic alignment.

Figure 7. Automatic detection of planes is shown in this image of our hardware lab. The range data from the ceiling created the highest peak in the Hough transform, and by performing the inverse operation, we have highlighted the pixels that contributed to this plane with a cross-hatch pattern.

renovation [8]. The areas scanned were difficult to reach, apparently, as the scanning hardware was held hundreds of feet off the ground by a crane. Another example of acquiring as-built models is that of sets for Hollywood movies [7]. The Cyrax scanner was used to scan a cave set from the movie "Starship Troopers." 3D CAD models were produced, which allowed computer graphics artists to superimpose animations in the proper locations.

Forensic Recording. During a crime scene investigation, many photos are taken, and in some cases, the scene is frozen or even disassembled and reassembled elsewhere for the duration of the legal process. All of this is done to allow the participants to re-examine the site to determine what happened.

This is a case where a static imagery of range and color is exactly what is needed. There is no need for dynamic data collection. It is also a case where the measurements need to be very accurate.

Remanufacturing. A range scanner from the Canadian National Research Council has a high accuracy and real-time acquisition rates device that captures range over a limited volume [2]. The error in range is 10–100 microns, the maximum scanning rate is 10 million samples per second, and the volume is a cube several centimeters on a side at a distance of some tens of centimeters. The high-accuracy of such a system makes it ideal for scanning an existing part with the goal of reproducing that part, especially when used with a CCM milling machine to accurately place the device.

Remote Walk-Through. The K^{2}T company has demonstrated, in conjunction with the Robotics Institute at CMU, the ability to build remote walk-throughs [8]. They scanned an abandoned research facility, collected color images, and also videotaped a helicopter fly-over of the site to reconstruct the surrounding topology. The result is a model that can be viewed from arbitrary locations.

3D Movies and Television. A obvious use of dense range data is the creation of true 3D movies where a viewer could move to any position desired to view the movie. This is in contrast to the so-called 3D movies that are stereo projections that give the user a 3D view from the camera's location. This application requires real-time range acquisition as well as hardware acceleration to display the images in real-time. Research in this area is underway at CMU's Robotics Institute [14].

In its fullest form, a viewer could walk anywhere and look in any direction, viewing a properly reconstructed scene. For sports broadcasts, the freedom of motion holds immense appeal, in that a viewer could be on the field or court with the players, moving with the action.

Of course, movie and television directors have made their careers choosing the best presentation for the viewers, and are bestowed with awards when they do this well. To preserve this, the viewer might be restrained to a small volume, but still be allowed to move, gaining a true sense of the 3D nature of the scene.

8. Conclusions

We are excited about building a successful range acquisition system, and the success of our system has been shown by the desire of others to use the data in their projects. As a custom system, we are able to quickly adapt our data collection methods to that required by different projects, an advantage not found in commercial systems. We feel in our own work and in the work of others that there is a large future for dense range data.

The ability to match color data with range data has also been successful, although fraught with significant processing requirements. The combined data enables realistic walk-throughs of real environments that would be far too complex (or impossible) to model.

9. Future Work

Our immediate goals for the future have to do with reliable automatic registration methods, and better calibration of the rangefinder system. We are also exploring the development of hardware devices that will allow the simultaneous collection of range and color data.

Our future work is narrow compared to all that could be done to provide better support for dense range images with color. Obviously, real-time acquisition hardware from multiple locations would increase the demand for real-time rendering, so hardware acceleration both in acquisition and rendering are important areas to explore, despite the difficulty involved. The large number of points is, in itself, a demand for faster rendering hardware. In addition, dealing with view-dependent artifacts such as specular highlights could be explored (and has been [25]), where recovery of the surface properties could be performed to more realistically yield the artifacts.

References

[1] Image-based rendering at unc. http://www.cs.unc.edu/~ibr/, 1999.

[2] J.-A. Beraldin, M. Rioux, F. Blais, J. Domey, and L. Cournoyer. Registered range and intensity imaging at 10-mega samples per second. *Opt. Eng.*, 31(1):88–94, 1992.

[3] P. J. Besl and N. D. McKay. A method for registration of 3-d shapes. *IEEE PAMI*, 14(2):239–256, 1992.

[4] P. E. Debevec and J. Malik. Recovering high dynamic range radiance maps from photographs. In *SIGGRAPH '97*, pages 369–178, Los Angeles, 1997.

[5] J. Eyles, S. Molnar, J. Poulton, T. Greer, A. Lastra, N. England, and L. Westover. Pixelflow: The realization. In *SIGGRAPH/Eurographics Workshop on Graphics Hardware*, pages 57–68, Los Angeles, CA, 1997.

[6] S. J. Gortler, R. Grzeszczuk, R. Szeliski, and M. F. Cohen. The lumigraph. In *SIGGRAPH 96*, 1996.

[7] C. Inc. The cyrax 3d laser imaging system. http://www.cyra.com/, 1999.

[8] K^2T. K^2T home page. http://www.k2t.com/, 1999.

[9] D. McAllister, L. Nyland, V. Popescu, A. Lastra, and C. McCue. Real-time rendering of real world environments. Technical TR99-019, UNC Computer Science, 1999.

[10] C. McCue. Multi-function point viewer. http://www.cs.unc.edu/~ibr/projects/multiple, 1999.

[11] L. McMillan. *An Image-based Approach to Three-Dimensional Computer Graphics*. Ph.d. dissertation, University of North Carolina at Chapel Hill, 1997. also available as UNC Technical Report TR97-013.

[12] L. McMillan and G. Bishop. Plenoptic modeling: An image-based rendering system. In *Proceedings of SIGGRAPH 95*, pages 39–46, Los Angeles, CA, 1995.

[13] G. Meenakshisundaram and S. Krishnan. A fast and efficient projection based approach for surface reconstruction. Technical Report TR99-023, UNC Computer Science, 1999.

[14] P. J. Narayanan, P. W. Rander, and T. Kanade. Constructing virtual worlds using dense stereo. In *Proceedings of Sixth IEEE International Conference on Computer Vision (ICCV'98)*, pages 3–10, Bombay, India, 1998.

[15] M. Oliveira. Ibr tiff file format. http://www.cs.unc.edu/~ibr/src/ibr_tifflib/, 1997.

[16] M. M. Oliveira and G. Bishop. Image-based objects. In *Interactive 3D*, Atlanta, GA, 1999.

[17] D. Perception. Manufacturers of innovative devices and software for the intelligent control of sensors and sensor processing. http://www.dperception.com/, 1998.

[18] P. Rademacher. Range image registration via consistency of empty space. http://www.cs.unc.edu/~ibr/projects/emptyspace/, 1999.

[19] P. Rademacher and G. Bishop. Multiple-center-of-projection images. In *SIGGRAPH98*, Orlando, FL, 1998.

[20] R. Raskar, G. Welch, M. Cutts, A. Lake, L. Stesin, and H. Fuchs. The office of the future: A unified approach to image-based modeling and spatially immersive displays. In *SIGGRAPH98*, pages 179–188, Orlando, FL, 1998.

[21] A. Research. Acuity research scanners and sensors. http://www.acuityresearch.com/, 1998.

[22] J. Shade, S. Gortler, L.-w. Hey, and R. Szeliski. Layered depth images. In *SIGGRAPH 98*, Orlando, FL, 1998.

[23] R. Y. Tsai. An efficient and accurate camera calibration technique for 3d machine vision. In *Proceedings of IEEE Conference on Computer Vision and Pattern Recognition*, pages 364–374, Miami Beach, FL, 1986.

[24] T. S. Yoo and J. M. Coggins. Using statistical pattern recognition techniques to control variable conductance diffusion. In H. H. Barrett and A. F. Gmitro, editors, *Information Processing in Medical Imaging (Lecture Notes in Computer Science 687)*, pages 495–471, Berlin, 1993. Springer-Verlag. Also available as UNC Technical Report TR94-047.

[25] Y. Yu, P. Debevec, J. Malik, and T. Hawkins. Inverse global illumination: Recovering reflectance models of real scenes from photographs. In *SIGGRAPH 99*, August 1999.

Object Modeling using Tomography and Photography

David T. Gering
MIT Artificial Intelligence Laboratory
Cambridge, MA 02139
gering@ai.mit.edu

William M. Wells III
Harvard Medical School and Brigham and
Women's Hospital, and
MIT Artificial Intelligence Laboratory
sw@ai.mit.edu

Abstract

This paper explores techniques for constructing a 3D computer model of an object from the real world by applying tomographic methods to a sequence of photographic images. While some existing methods can better handle occlusion and concavities, the techniques proposed here have the advantageous capability of generating very high-resolution models with attractive speed and simplicity. The application of these methods is presently limited to an appropriate class of mostly convex objects with Lambertian surfaces. The results are volume rendered or surface rendered to produce an interactive display of the object with near life-like realism.

1 Introduction

This paper addresses the problem of reconstructing an object from its images and rendering it from novel viewpoints. Virtualized reality, introduced by Kanade, Narayanan, and Rander [4,7], has applications from animated movies, to interactive education, to exchanging information on the World Wide Web. Creating virtual representations of real-world scenes departs from the conventional stereo correspondence problem in that information must be gathered and integrated from all sides of the scene.

This paper describes how tomography can be used to create a model of a 3D object and render it with near life-like realism, as demonstrated in Figure 1. Tomography refers to the process of forming cross-sectional images of an object by illuminating it from many different directions. Radon [8] first solved the problem of reconstructing an object from its projections in 1917. The field of medical imaging was revolutionized when Hounsfield invented the x-ray computed tomographic (CT) scanner for which he shared the Nobel prize in 1972. The output of a CT scan is a map of x-ray attenuation coefficients which offers doctors a view of internal organs. The new application considered here differs from

diagnostic medicine in that the object being imaged is opaque.

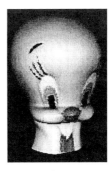

Figure 1: Example of a color, 3D model created using the methods described here.

We propose applying tomographic techniques to conventional photographic and video imagery. There are a variety of tomographic reconstruction methods. This paper applies a type of simple backprojection and suggests that more methods form the history of tomography are relevant to forming reconstructions from photographic images. For example, it may become necessary to have less restricted camera trajectories, which has already been studied by Horn [3].

2 Related work

Early work by Bolles, Baker, and Marimont [1] proposed constructing an epipolar-plane image which is simpler to analyze than a large set of images. Mellor, Teller, and Lozano-Perez [6] extended their approach to work with arbitrary camera positions and some forms of occlusion. Contour-based methods were applied by Szeliski [13] and Seales and Faugeras [11]. One approach explored here is similar to these in that it employs silhouettes such as Szeliszki does, yet it avoids the complexity of using octrees. Our techniques share similarities with the recent approaches that have turned away from stereo methods to use first principles. Collins [2] digitized scene space into voxels that are traversed and

11

colored. Seitz and Dyer [10] furthered this approach with a voxel coloring algorithm to handle occlusion. Szeliski and Golland [12] also handle occlusion by way of an ordering technique as they simultaneously find disparities, true colors and opacities. Some approaches explored in this work differ from the other volumetric approaches approaches in that there is no thresholding or segmentation until *after* the volume has been reconstructed.

The tomographic methods explored here have difficulty handling occlusion and concavities. However, for an appropriate class of mostly convex objects, these techniques are attractive for their speed and simplicity. The setup and calibration are fast and easy, and the equipment is simple, inexpensive, and commonplace. The algorithm scales linearly in the number of views and is very computationally inexpensive when compared with the other techniques. Best of all, the resulting images look pleasing and have very high resolution. The image on the previous page was reconstructed using 4.6 million voxels in 8 minutes on a Pentium II, 266MHz machine. For comparison, Seitz and Dyer state that their voxel coloring algorithm reconstructs 53,000 voxels in 95 seconds. If we could assume linear scaling, computing 4.6 million voxels would take 134 minutes.

3   Method

3.1 Data acquisition

In medical imaging, the patient lies on a table while the x-ray source and detector spin about. We took the easier approach of revolving the object of interest on a milling machine rotary table in view of a fixed camera and light source.

A pullnix color CCD camera was affixed with a FUJI 75 mm lens (long enough to assume orthographic projection) positioned 93 inches from the object. The object was a plastic representation of Tweety Bird in front of a black background. The scene was irradiated with a spotlight reflected off a white panel directly behind the camera. 180 color pictures of size 160x180 were taken over 360 degrees of rotation. Samples are shown in Figure 2.

3.2 The radon transform

The Radon transform, *P(θ,d)*, of a function, *f(x,y)*, is computed by forming a projection of the function for each of many views, θ. For a given projection, *P(θ)*, the value at location *d*, *P(θ,d)*, is determined by the line integral through *f(x,y)* along a ray. This ray makes an angle, θ, with the x-axis, and the ray stands a distance, *d*, from a parallel ray through the origin. Hence, the origin projects

onto *d=0*. This relationship can be written using a delta function as:

$$P(\theta,d) = \int_{-\infty}^{\infty}\int_{-\infty}^{\infty} f(x,y)\delta(x\cos\theta + y\sin\theta - d)dxdy$$

Figure 3 demonstrates this graphically.

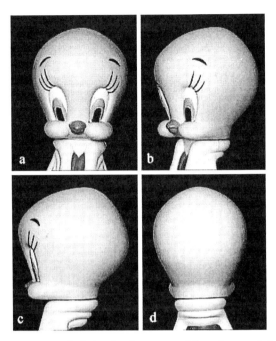

Figure 2: Original photographic views, (a) through (d), are taken at 0, 50, 90, and 180 degrees, respectively.

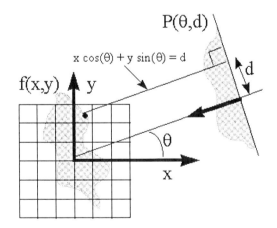

Figure 3: Computation of the radon transform.

3.3 The modified radon transform

A sequence of photographic images can be thought of as a modified Radon transform that differs in being discrete and operating on opaque data. Each image is taken at a different view angle, θ. Each row of an image is a projection through an axial slice of the object of interest. Projections are vertically stacked to form a 3D modified Radon transform. Each pixel of each row has a value determined by a photographic detector horizontally located a distance, d, from the center of the lens.

The line integrals in the Radon transform become something else in the modified version. For translucent objects, the detectors *see* the result of compositing the color and opacity of volume elements, or voxels, in the order they are encountered along the ray from the object to the camera. For opaque objects, such as our Tweety Bird, each detector receives the scene radiance of a surface patch on the object.

Tomographic methods would ideally be applied under ambient lighting conditions. Patches of a Lambertian surface have a hemispherical radiation pattern with brightness proportional to the cosine of the angle between the view ray and the surface normal. This effect is cancelled by foreshortening so that different views receive identical brightness information from a given portion of the surface. However, one goal of our work is to model objects as simply and inexpensively as possible. Given this constraint, ambient lighting conditions are not always possible, and we used diffuse lighting. In a diffuse lighting model, the power irradiating a surface patch falls off with the cosine of the angle between the incident light ray and the surface normal. (Since the light source was positioned directly behind the camera in or case, we can refer to the view angle and the angle of incidence interchangeably.) Each non-occluded surface patch makes a brightness contribution to the modified Radon transform in the half of all views which see its front side.

Diffuse lighting also introduces artifacts into the final reconstruction. Consider the fact that we implement tomography by spinning the object about one axis. Surface normals have an axial component and a vertical component. Patches that are more vertically oriented will contribute less to the modified Radon transform, and this will appear as an artifact in a reconstruction because more vertically oriented patches will be darker.

For shiny surfaces, incident light reflects about the surface normal at an angle equal to the angle of incidence, just as seen in a mirror. When this angle of reflection coincides with the viewing angle, a bright spot appears as specular reflection. Therefore, if a patch is shiny, then specular highlights will appear in the modified Radon transform. This leads to artifacts in the final reconstruction, because the highlights will be fixed rather than varying with the viewing angle of the observer who is exploring the reconstructed object.

Putting these two, small artifacts aside for the remainder of the discussion, call the axial component of a patch's surface normal, θ_n, the angle of incident light, θ_i, and the patch's brightness, I. If the patch is small enough to be seen by only one detector at a time, then the patch's total contribution to the modified Radon transform is:

$$\sum_{\theta_v=0}^{360} MAX\left(I * \cos\left(\theta_i - \theta_n\right), 0\right)$$

We will later refer to $\theta_i - \theta_n$ as φ.

3.4 Backprojection

Object reconstruction becomes a task of inverting the modified Radon transform. Refer again to Figure 3 to observe how we can recover the function, *f(x,y)*. Each *P(θ)* can be projected back onto the x-y grid, thus earning the name *backprojection*. The pixel with a black dot (located at x=1, y=3) can be recovered by computing the value of d from the angle, θ, and the coordinates, *x* and *y*, from the ray equation:

$$x\cos\left(\theta\right) + y\sin\left(\theta\right) = d$$

Then, *d* is used to index into *P(θ)* to obtain a value, *P(θ,d)*, to assign to the pixel. This process is repeated for each view, and the values are summed to accumulate one aggregate pixel value.

3.5 Filtered backprojection

Suppose *f(x,y)* is an impulse of density at the origin. Then, each image will contribute a ray of brightness that emanates from the center of the image and intersects the center of the reconstruction. The composite reconstruction will appear much like a bunch of bright spokes intersecting at the center. In the limit of infinitely many views, the reconstruction will approach a *1/r* distribution, where *r* is the distance from the origin.

If we view the image collection process and (unfiltered) backprojection together as a linear system, we see that the impulse response is *1/r*, and because the components of the system are linear (and shift-invariant), the response of the system to an arbitrary density will be a convolution of that density by *1/r*.

Ideally, we would prefer the impulse response of our imaging and reconstruction to be close to a delta function. To obtain this, we could post-filter the reconstruction with a filter that has been designed to be an implementation of the inverse of *1/r* — this would be *a de-blurring* or *de-convolution* approach to the problem. It turns out that in this situation, some efficiency may be gained by using a suitable filter in the images before they are backprojected — this is the standard *filtered backprojection* (FBP) approach.

It is useful to observe that the standard filters used in the first step of FBP are essentially high-pass filters. Therefore, they may be also viewed as edge-enhancing filters, and then FBP may be summarized *as edge-enhance, then backproject.*

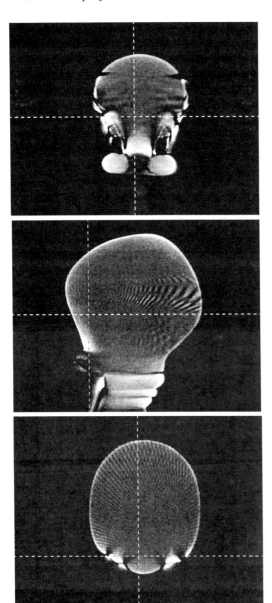

Figure 4: Cross sections of reconstructed density using filtered backprojection.

We employed a 1D filtering kernel prior to backprojection. The kernel is due to Ramachandran et al. [9], uses linear interpolation, and has the form:

$$k(0) = 1/4$$

$$k(i) = \begin{cases} \dfrac{-1}{(\pi i)^2}, & odd\ i \\ 0, & even\ i \end{cases}$$

The results of FBP reconstruction are shown in Figure 4 (the contrast of the images has been adjusted for viewing). It is a 3D volume containing a representation of the object as an intensity density. In this example, the object appears as a bright region embedded in a dark volume. In the reconstruction, the bright region is shaped like the original 3D object. The surface of the object appears as a prominently bright shell, and the brightness of the shell is modulated by the brightness of the original object. For example, in the coronal cross section, which has been chosen to intersect the reconstruction in the region of the face, the bright and dark areas of the eyes are clearly visible.

3.6 A new filter for backprojection

Figure 2a-d shows samples of the original photographs. There is a modified Radon transform image for each axial slice of Tweety. Figure 5a shows the Radon transform for one slice through Tweety's eyes. Each row of the image is a projection for a view, or $P(\theta)$, and each column is a d.

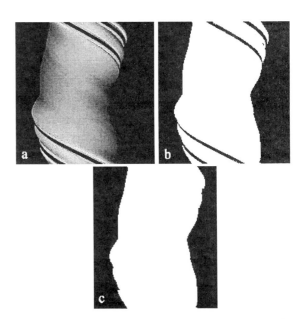

Figure 5: Radon transform (a). Image (b) is derived from applying a threshold to (a) just above the background noise floor. Image (c) is derived from filling the gaps along each row of (b).

Figure 6a shows the unfiltered backprojection of the first row of 5a. Figure 6b adds the backprojection of the middle row. Observe how the yellow color of the back of Tweety's head has overwritten the blue and black color of his eyes. The eye color is still apparent, yet it has lost its original brilliant saturation by being averaged with *intruder colors* that do not belong at that location on the x-y grid.

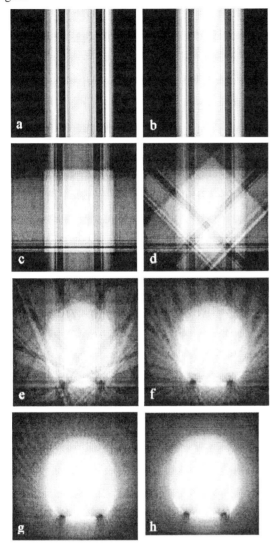

Figure 6: Images (a) through (h), are tomographic reconstructions using 1, 2, 4, 8, 16, 32, 64, and 180 equally spaced views, respectively.

The process continues unfolding in Figure 6c, which is a tomographic reconstruction from 4 equally spaced views. Observe that the blue and black color of surface patches in the eyes are still seen from the side views, but the patches experience foreshortening. Figure 6 demonstrates that the shape of the object emerges in as

few as 16 views, but shape and color accuracy continue improving as more views are added.

During backprojection, a pixel corresponding to a surface patch on Tweety, receives back its contribution to the Radon transform from the views which saw it as expressed earlier in equation form. However, the other half of the views also contribute *intruder colors* to the pixel. The pixel's color becomes averaged with the average color seen by that pixel's detector in the other half of the views. The end result (Figure 6h) is a reconstruction of both the object's shape and texture situated in a *tomographic fog*.

A correct inverse modified Radon transform will assign each pixel the exact value that it contributed to the transform. We can dissipate the fog and block intruder colors by stopping the projections from views that do not see the patch. However, an accurate inverse modified Radon transform is not desired! When the absolute value of the difference between the angle of incident light and the axial component of the surface normal, $|\varphi|$, is large (near 90 degrees), the patch is seen to be darker by the detector. Therefore, the patch's contribution to the modified Radon transform is darker than the patch itself, and this will result in a 3D model with muted colors.

We can correct for both problems simultaneously by weighting each backprojection by $cos(\varphi)$. However, the surface normals are not initially known. This suggests a two-pass algorithm where the first pass uses standard filtered backprojection to recover the object. The surface normals are then computed from the reconstruction, and then filtered backprojection is re-implemented with a different filter for each φ.

3.7 Rendering the reconstruction

The end goal of this work is a realistic graphics rendering of the object. Filtered backprojection of all three color components of the data provides a 3D volume of object texture. The data can be visualized through volume rendering. Consider the 2D output image to be a window into the scene. For each pixel in the window, a ray is cast into the scene, and a color value can be assigned to the pixel using one of a variety of methods. Maximum Intensity Projection (MIP) [14] colors the pixel with the maximum intensity found along the ray. Composite rendering composites colors that the ray passes through according to the opacity values of those voxels, and the order in which the ray encounters them.

Either method encounters trouble with Tweety Bird. The black eyes are nearly indistinguishable from the dark surroundings, so MIP colors the eyes with the yellow color from the back of Tweety's head. Composite rendering requires opacity information.

Figure 7 shows a MIP of the reconstructed intensities from a viewpoint that was chosen to be below the plane of the views of the input data. In this preliminary experiment, the front/back surface issue was handled by manually suppressing the rear half of the intensity data. The purpose of this experiment is to demonstrate that useful surface brightness information is present in the reconstruction, yet the filtering has introduced highlight and shadow artifacts most pronounced around the eyebrows, which are high-frequency texture. Consequently, the next renderings were generated from reconstructions that result from unfiltered backprojection.

Figure 7: MIP of filtered, backprojected reconstruction from novel viewpoint.

3.8 Recovering opacity

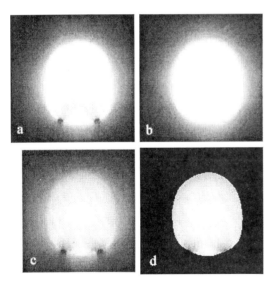

Figure 8: Image (a) is an opacity map derived from backprojecting (5.b). Image (b) is derived from (5.c) to assign non-zero opacity to the eyeballs. Image (c) is one slice of the reconstruction, while image (d) is the same slice rendered using the opacity information in (b).

To aid the rendering process, a second backprojection (but with only a single color component: gray) was performed to create an opacity map to complement the reconstructed texture map. The Radon transforms were automatically thresholded just above the noise floor of the background, as shown in Figure 5.c.

A reconstruction made from this filtered transform is shown in Figure 8.a, where the eyeballs do not exist. Using the assumption of a mostly convex object, the threshold operation was modified to fill in gaps. The resulting Radon transform shown in Figure 5.d was used to reconstruct the opacity map of Figure 8.b.

The color and opacity information form a 4-component volume that can be used successfully for rendering. Figure 8.c and 8.d show a rendering of the unfiltered, one-pass reconstructed slice with and without using opacity information to segment the image.

4 Results

In an effort to perform object modeling in the most computationally inexpensive way, renderings were made from the unfiltered, single-pass backprojection with the help of the opacity map.

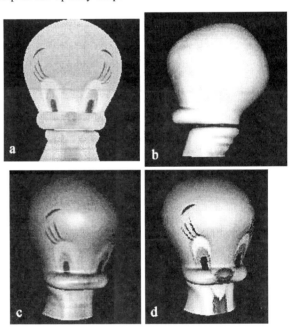

Figure 9: Image (a) is a volume rendering using intensity projection of texture from (8.c) and the opacity information from (8.b). Image (b) is a surface model of the opacity map in (8.b). Image (c) is the surface model of (b) with the texture from the backprojected reconstruction (8.c). Image (d) is similar, except the texture is taken from the original photographic images (2).

4.1 Volume rendering

Figure 9.a shows an intensity projection made from casting rays through the opacity information until a voxel is encountered with a opacity greater than 90% of full. Then the color values were taken from that voxel.

The flat result is a nature of intensity projection. More beautiful results can be obtained by computing the surface normals of the opacity map and applying a lighting model to shade the object. This technique was performed with the surface rendering described below.

4.2 Surface rendering

An alternative to visualizing our reconstructed volumes through ray-casting is to construct a surface model as a collection of triangles. The Marching Cubes algorithm [5] was run on the opacity map to extract the surface. Marching Cubes can be thought of as creating a polygon that intersects each voxel where the volume's scalar data crosses a threshold, such as opacity being 90% of full value. Figure 9.b shows a 3D rendering of the Tweety's surface. Figure 9.c colored each triangle vertex using the color components from the unfiltered backprojection, and the surface normals from the opacity map. Figure 10 shows a close-up of the many triangles that comprise Tweety's surface.

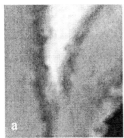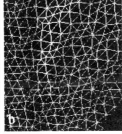

Figure 10: Image (a) is a close-up view of the eye of (9.d). Image (b) is a wire frame representation.

4.3 Projected texture

Figure 9.d is the most life-like representation of Tweety. The surface model described above was colored by computing the axial component of each surface normal. The angle of this vector was used to select the original photographic image with the closest view angle. (Equivalently, a row was selected from the modified Radon transform for this axial slice). Then the detector, d, which observed the vertex in this view was computed from the ray equation described earlier. The vertex's color could then be taken from $P(\theta,d)$.

This process is effectively performing backprojection with a delta function that selects the view that saw a

surface patch most directly. Thus, unconcluded patches are recovered with their fully saturated brightness.

$$\sum_{\theta_v=0}^{360} \delta\left(\theta_i - \theta_n\right)\left(I * \cos\left(\theta_i - \theta_n\right)\right)$$

4.4 Future work

Figure 9.d appears a little rough due to inaccuracies in the computation of the surface normals. Errors could be averaged out by modifying the above equation to weight a number of views that observed the patch most directly. Future work can similarly use the opacity map to assign weights to eliminate occluded views. The occlusion in some types of objects could be handled by performing tomography about two different axis of rotation. Furthermore, another class of tomographic techniques [15] offers algebraic reconstruction techniques (ART) as an iterative alternative to backprojection.

5 Summary

This paper presents an analysis of how tomography could offer a simple, computationally inexpensive solution to recovering an object's shape and texture from multiple views. These techniques apply best to objects that are mostly convex, opaque, and with Lambertian surfaces. Under these circumstances, the algorithms produce nice-looking, very high-resolution results in a comparatively short time.

References

[1]   R. C. Bolles and H. H. Baker and D. H. Marimont. Epipolar-Plane Image Analysis: An Approach to Determining Structure from Motion. *International Journal of Computer Vision.* 1(7):7-55, 1987.

[2]   R. Collins. A space-sweep approach to true multi-image matching.   *Proc. Computer vision and Pattern Recognition Conf.,* 358-363, 1996.

[3]   B. K. P. Horn. Density Reconstruction using Arbitrary Ray-Sampling Schemes. *Proceedings of the IEEE,* 66(5):551-562, May, 1978.

[4]   T. Kanade, P. J. Narayanan, P. W. Rander. Virtualized Reality: Concepts and Early Results. *IEEE Workshop on the Representation of Visual Scenes.* Boston, June 24, 1995.

[5]   W. E. Lorensen and H. E. Cline. Marching Cubes: A High Resolution 3D Surface Construction Algorithm. *Computer Graphics* 21(3):163-169, July 1987.

[6]   J. P. Mellor, S. Teller, and Thomas Lozano-Perez. Dense Depth Maps from Epipolar Images. Technical Report 1593. MIT Artificial Intelligence Laboratory, 1996.

[7]   P. J. Narayanan and P. W. Rander and T. Kanade. Constructing Virtual Worlds Using Dense Stereo.

Proceedings of the 6th International Conference on Computer Vision. Bombay, 3-10, 1998.

[8] J. Radon. Uber die Bestimmung von Funktionen durch ihre Integralwerte angs gewisser Mannigfaltigkeiter. *Berichte Sachsische Akademie der Wissenschaften*, Leipzig, Math. — Phys. Kl. 69:262-267, 1917.

[9] G. N. Ramachandran and A. V. Lakshminarayanan. Three Dimensional Reconstruction from Radiographs and Electron Micrographs: Applications of Convolutions Instead of Fourier Transforms. *Proc. Natl. Acad. Sci. USA*, 68:2236-2240, 1971.

[10] S. M. Seitz and C. M. Dyer. Photorealistic scene reconstruction by space coloring. *IEEE Computer society Conference on Computer Vision and Pattern Recognition (CVPR '97)*, San Juan, Puerto Rico, June 1997.

[11] W. Seales and O. Faugeras. Building three-dimensional object models from image sequences. *CVGIP: Image Understanding*, 3(61):308-324, 1995.

[12] R. Szeliski and P. Golland. Stereo Matching with Transparency and Matting. *Proceedings of the 6th International Conference on Computer Vision*. Bombay, 1998.

[13] R. Szeliski. Rapid octree construction from image sequences. CVGIP: *Image Understanding*. 1(58):23-32, 1993.

[14] U. Tiede and K.H. Hohne et al. Investigation of Medical 3D-Rendering Algorithms. *IEEE Computer Graphcs Applications*, pages 41-51, March 1990.

[15] S. Webb. *The Physics of Medical Imaging*. Institue of Physics Publishing. London, 1988.

Session II

Structure-from-Motion
and Calibration

Multi-View 3D Estimation and Applications to Match Move

Harpreet S. Sawhney Y. Guo J. Asmuth Rakesh Kumar

Sarnoff Corporation, CN5300, Princeton, NJ 08530 hsawhney@sarnoff.com

Abstract

Multiple views of a rigid 3D scene captured from a moving camera can be used to estimate the 3D poses (rotations and translations) and the 3D structure of the unmodeled scene. In this problem domain, there are two key problems addressed in this paper: (i) automatic Euclidean pose estimation in extended sequences even when views of the scene rapidly change, that is features come in and go out of view relatively rapidly, and (ii) insertion of synthetic 3D objects in the real scene and their authentic projection into the given real views (also called Match Move*). The paper presents a number of examples of different camera motions to highlight the versatility of 3D estimation. Examples of match move are also presented.*

1 Introduction

Applications involving synthesis [10, 16] of real scenes and synthetic objects require image analysis tools that help in automating the synthesis process. One such application area is *Match Move* in which the goal is to insert synthetic 3D objects in real but unmodeled scenes and create their views from the given camera positions so that they appear to move as if they were a part of the real scene. Insertion of synthetic objects can be done in 2D also, for instance in broadcast applications for billboard insertion [12], however, in this paper we focus on the problem of 3D insertion.

Seamless 3D insertion requires tools to allow the user to situate the synthetic objects with respect to real surfaces. Subsequently the objects need to be projected from all the given camera viewpoints. In order to automate this process, it is required that the situating of the objects be done in as few frames as possible, typically one, and all the other views be created automatically. For placement of the objects with respect to the real scene, accurate albeit limited 3D geometry is required, for instance, estimation of local surface patches may suffice. For stable 3D appearance change of the object from the given camera positions, reliable 3D camera pose computation is required. Note that in this work we are not attempting to create novel views of the real scene, only real views of the real and the synthetic scene. Furthermore, since the graphics objects are typically created in an Euclidean world, it is strongly desirable that the real scene and the poses be represented using Euclidean coordinates. Therefore, an important ingredient for *Match Move* is a reliable computation of Euclidean poses and 3D geometry over *extended* image sequences or videos of unmodeled arbitrary scenes. Stability of pose computation over extended sequences is required to avoid jitter and drift in the location and appearance of synthetic objects with respect to the real scene.

Multi-view pose and geometry analysis has attracted much attention in the past few years ([8, 9, 4] to cite a few). A number of papers have been devoted to projective, affine and Euclidean estimation. However, pose estimation under extended camera motions has not received enough attention. Most of the work on extended sequences has used a fixation type camera motion, that is, a motion in which features are kept into view continuously for a large number of frames [9, 4]. However, for *Match Move* and related applications, extended scene capture with motions in which features appear and disappear relatively rapidly are quite common.

This paper presents algorithms for automated end-to-end multi-view pose and geometry estimation that work with weak or strong calibration. The highlights of the algorithms are: (i) automatic multi-view feature tracking, (ii) initialization of pose and 3D geometry based on local collection of frames, and (iii) computation of global poses and 3D geometry by iterative bundle block adjustment. A number of quantitative results for different camera motions are presented in which re-projection errors of points are shown. The contrast in the magnitude of re-projection errors between local estimates and global estimates is shown. This is similar to the work on local-to-global pose and appearance (estimation) for static but pan-tilt-zoom cameras [13, 17]. The stability of multi-view estimation is further highlighted by situating synthetic objects in one frame and re-projecting these over all the frames. Unfortunately, visual evaluation of jitter and drift for synthetic insertion cannot be done in the print media. However, detailed visual results will be shown in our presentation using video and VRML formats. In summary, the main contributions of the paper are a local-to-global 3D estimation algorithm that produces stable poses for long sequences, and demonstration of jitter and drift free insertion of synthetics into the real scene based on the computed poses.

Figure 1: Three frames (1,21,32) of the 32-frame *garden* sequence.

Figure 2: Three frames (1,8,15) of the 15-frame *dorm* sequence.

2 Problem Formulation & Approach

Given a video sequence of N frames, the problem is to compute the camera poses (the rotations and translations) without the knowledge of the 3D model and with some rough knowledge of the internal parameters of the camera. The approach should work with a variety of different 3D camera motions, especially those in which novel parts of the scene appear and disappear relatively rapidly. Of course, imaging scenarios in which features remain fairly persistent, as in fixated motions, are also naturally handled. A sparse collection of 3D features are also computed in the process of pose computation. However, in this work we do not attempt a dense 3D structure reconstruction. Multi-view pose estimation is an important first step towards arbitrary topology dense scene reconstruction [14, 3]. In general, the problems of correspondence over the sequence, camera pose and 3D structure estimation, and camera calibration estimation are tied together. Solving all the problems in a single optimization problem is complex and will in general not lead to stable and correct solutions. Therefore, we adopt a strategy of progressive complexity with feedback in which earlier stages work on smaller segments of the data and generate inputs for the latter stages.

We divide the problem into the following different steps:

1. Frame-to-frame patch tracking that allows new features to emerge and older features to disappear.

2. Pairwise estimation of camera poses with elimination of outliers in the feature tracks.

3. Computation of camera poses for overlapping subsequences with pairwise estimates as initial guesses.

4. Representation of longer sequences in a consistent coordinate system using pose consistency across the overlapping subsequences.

5. Global bundle block adjustment to compute the maximum likelihood estimate of camera poses.

6. Match move generation using the poses and limited 3D structure estimation.

2.1 Feature Tracking

We exploit the frame-to-frame coherence of video sequences for establishing good correspondences between pairs of frames. Since we do not want to rely on the assumption of presence of specific structures in the scene, and also want to handle fairly arbitrary 3D motions, we employ a combination of strategies to choose and track features. The first step is to choose new features in every new frame. Features are chosen on the basis of their contrast strength and distinctiveness with respect to their local neighborhoods. The distinctiveness property is useful for selecting features in scenes where there may be a lot of repetitive structures and hence establishing unique correspondences may be a problem.

Salient point features are selected as centers of patches whose auto-correlation surface satisfies a number of properties at a few different scales. Auto-correlation surfaces are computed at those locations where the average gradient magnitude within a window is above a chosen threshold (typically chosen to be 10.0). At each scale in a Gaussian pyramid, the auto-correlation surface must satisfy the following properties: (i) it should be approximated well by a quadratic surface, (ii) it should be concave downwards, (iii) the minimum curvature magnitude should be above a threshold, and (iv) the ratio of the larger to the smaller curvature should be above a threshold. Checking these properties at a number of given scales ensures that high contrast points that are locally distinctive are selected. The specific thresholds used to select the initial feature points are not very critical since a number of processing stages are used to prune and further constrain good features to track.

In every new frame feature points are initialized as above and the features from a previous frame are projected into the new frame. Since neither the camera pose nor the 3D location of the features is known, both forward and reverse displacement fields are computed between pair t and $t + 1$ of frames. The displacement field is computed using a multi-resolution coarse-to-fine algorithm like that of Lucas-Kanade and Bergen et al. [11, 2]. It may also be computed by constraining the displacements using a small-motion 3D model as in Hanna et al. [5]. The forward and backward displacement vectors are used to check for flow consistency at a point. That is, a point is considered good if its predicted location using the forward and backward flow projection is consistent. That is, point $\mathbf{p}_t$ is flow consistent if $\delta(\mathbf{p}_t) = \|\mathbf{p}_{pred} - \mathbf{p}_t\| \leq \epsilon$, where $\mathbf{p}_{pred} = \mathbf{p}^+ + \mathbf{ub}_{t+1}(\mathbf{p}^+)$, $\mathbf{p}^+ = \mathbf{p}_t + \mathbf{uf}_t(\mathbf{p}_t)$, $\mathbf{p}^+$ is the forward projection of $\mathbf{p}_t$ into the frame $t + 1$ using the forward displacement field $\mathbf{uf}_t$, and $\mathbf{p}_{pred}$ is the backward projection of $\mathbf{p}^+$ into frame t using the backward displacement field $\mathbf{ub}_{t+1}$. Note that $\mathbf{ub}_{t+1}(\mathbf{p}^+)$ is an interpolated vector since $\mathbf{p}^+$ may not in general lie on a grid location.

In any given frame both new points and points projected from a previous frame are checked for flow consistency at their locations. Points that are flow consistent are kept for further tracking. The process of instantiation of new points, projection of previous points into a new frame and flow consistency checks is repeated over the whole sequence to obtain multi-frame point tracks.

2.2 Pairwise Camera Pose Estimation

Initial estimates for the camera poses are computed using the fundamental matrix constraint. The tri-focal constraint could have been used as well [19]. Given a point $\mathbf{P}_w$ in some world coordinate system, its projec-

tion in the fth frame can be written as:

$$\mathbf{p}_f \approx A M_f \mathbf{P}_w \qquad (1)$$

where $A = \begin{bmatrix} \begin{bmatrix} f_x & 0 & 0 \end{bmatrix}^T & \begin{bmatrix} 0 & f_y & 0 \end{bmatrix}^T & \begin{bmatrix} c_x & c_y & 1 \end{bmatrix}^T \end{bmatrix}$, is the camera calibration matrix with the scale factors and center coordinates in image pixels. $M_f = \begin{bmatrix} R_f & \mathbf{T}_f \\ \mathbf{0} & 1 \end{bmatrix}$, is the 3×4 camera projection matrix with the rotation and translation for frame f.

Given point correspondences between a pair of frames, it is well known that the two frame projection constraint is captured by the fundamental matrix constraint:

$$\mathbf{p}_f^T F \mathbf{p}_{f+1} = 0$$

The fundamental matrix can be computed by a number of known techniques. We employ Zhang's [21] algorithm that combines a linear method for initialization, and then refines it with a method that employs image based error minimization. Furthermore, outliers are rejected using a least median squares minimization. The final F matrix is computed using the image based error measure after outlier rejection.

With the knowledge of the approximately known calibration, the F matrix can be decomposed into the camera pose matrices M_f using the technique of Hartley [7]. Note that in principal, using multiple frames and projective camera matrices, the self-calibration techniques also could be employed. However, first, the stability of these techniques under arbitrary 3D motions is not guaranteed, and second, in practise we find that the only internal camera parameter that needs adjustment beyond the roughly known parameters is the focal length (or scale in pixel coordinates). Aspect ratio, skew and the principal point are either generally known or nominal parameters are adequate. Therefore, we assume standard values for these and use a rough initial guess of the focal length (in pixels) to convert from projective camera matrices to Euclidean. The focal length is adjusted further in the maximum-likelihood stage.

Figure 3: Three frames (1,11,21) of the 50-frame *Terrain* sequence.

2.3 From Pairwise Estimates to Subsequence Poses

For long sequences, for computational efficiency, the 3D estimation is divided into two stages. First, for a selected set of key frames, both the 3D pose estimates and the 3D coordinates of selected points in these frames are computed. Subsequently, using the 3D coordinates of the points, the poses of the in-between frames are computed. The key frames may be chosen using any of the following criteria : (i) regularly sub-sampled frames over time when the motion is relatively uniform and smooth, (ii) sub-sampled frames between which parallax motion is beyond a certain threshold, (iii) frames around which there is a change in the number of feature tracks, and (iv) user-specified frames. The description of 3D pose and point estimation that follows is applied to the key frames. Pose estimation for in-between frames is a subset of the complete 3D estimation problem, hence its description is left out.

In order to exploit the static rigid scene constraint, the pairwise camera estimates are used to create consistent camera pose estimates and the corresponding 3D point locations over short subsequences. The advantage of dividing the problem into subsequence estimates is threefold: (i) better computational efficiency since global bundle block adjustment for all frames is expensive, (ii) progressively better generation of estimates leading to a global maximum likelihood estimation, and (iii) limited build up of error due to small scale concatenation of local pose estimates (akin to [13, 17]).

Point tracks that persist for the time period of each subsequence are used to create the consistent estimates. For a subsequence 0 to s, say 0 is chosen as the reference frame. The pairwise camera estimation is done for each pair 0-f with $f \leq s$. Therefore, for each subsequence the camera transformations benefit from varying baseline between pairs of frames. For subsequence processing, the pairwise estimates first need to be represented consistently in the fth frame's coordinate system. This can be achieved by solving for an unknown scale factor for each frame. That is $\mathbf{P}_f = R_f \mathbf{P}_0 + \alpha_f \mathbf{T}_f$ where $\mathbf{P}_0$ and α_f are the unknowns, $\mathbf{P}_0$'s are the 3D points in the 0th frame and α_f is the scale factor for the fth frame in the subsequence. One of the α's is arbitrarily set to unity. The rest of the scale factors and all the 3D points can be solved by minimizing the image projection errors or the triangulation errors [6]. Essentially the sum of image reprojection errors, $\sum_n \sum_f \|\mathbf{p}_{fn} - \Pi(\mathbf{P}_{fn})\|^2$, is minimized over all 3D points and frames indexed by n and f, respectively, using iterative least squares [6]. (Π is the 3D to 2D projection operator). The output of this process is a collection of consistent camera poses and a set of reconstructed 3D points all of which are visible in the subsequence 0 to s.

However, the poses obtained above are not optimal since only the overall scale factors have been adjusted in the optimization process. In order to compute the maximum likelihood estimates for the camera poses and 3D points for the subsequence, a bundle block adjustment is applied. The following maximum likelihood criterion is minimized:

$$E = \sum_f \sum_n \left\| \frac{\mathbf{P_{0,n}} - \mathbf{T_f}}{\|\mathbf{P_{0,n}} - \mathbf{T_f}\|} - \mathbf{R_f} \cdot \frac{\mathbf{p_{f,n}}}{\|\mathbf{p_{f,n}}\|} \right\|^2$$

where $\mathbf{p_{f,n}} = \mathbf{\Pi}(\mathbf{P_{fn}})$ is the image projection operation expressed in homogeneous coordinates, and $\mathbf{P}_{fn} = \mathbf{R_f}\mathbf{P_{0,n}} + \mathbf{T_f}$ is the coordinate transformation of the nth point from the world to the fth camera coordinate system using the rotation and translation. Essentially the 3D points $\mathbf{P_{0,n}}$ are projected as unit vectors in the fth frame, and the corresponding observed image points, $\mathbf{p}_{f,n}$, are also represented as unit vectors. The error measure is the distance between the two unit vectors summed over all the 3D points and frames (including the reference frame) indexed by n and f, respectively. The advantage of this representation is that the images could each be a spherical mosaic representation. The unit vector representations can handle both planar and wide angle projections. The calibration parameters also are folded into the image vector, $\mathbf{p}_{f,n}$ as in Eqn. 1. Therefore, the focal length and other parameters can be adjusted within the same optimization.

Bundle block adjustment exploits the nice block structure that the system of normal equations has for the above sum of squares problem. The LHS matrix looks like:

$$\begin{bmatrix} \mathbf{M}_1 & & \mathbf{0} & & \mathbf{N}_{11} & \cdots & \mathbf{N}_{1,P} \\ & \ddots & & & \vdots & \ddots & \vdots \\ \mathbf{0} & & \mathbf{M}_{F-1} & & \mathbf{N}_{F-1,1} & \cdots & \mathbf{N}_{F-1,P} \\ \mathbf{N}_{11}^T & \cdots & \mathbf{N}_{F-1,1}^T & & \mathbf{S}_1 & & \mathbf{0} \\ \vdots & \ddots & \vdots & & & \ddots & \\ \mathbf{N}_{1,P}^T & \cdots & \mathbf{N}_{F-1,P}^T & & \mathbf{0} & & \mathbf{S}_P \end{bmatrix}$$

The $\mathbf{M}_f$'s are the Hessian matrices (with the standard approximation for a sum-of-squares problem [20]) with respect to the fth camera parameters, and thus represent the summation over all the points visible in frame f. Likewise, $\mathbf{S}_n$'s are the Hessians with respect to the the nth 3D point and are summed over all the frames in which that point is visible. The off-diagonal blocks, $\mathbf{N}_{f,n}$ matrices corresponding to the cross derivatives with respect to the fth frame and nth 3D point. Furthermore, the incremental solution for the 3D points can be analytically computed in terms of the solutions of the camera parameters. Therefore, by back-substitution, one never has to store the full $k*(F-1)+3*P$ matrix where k are the camera parameters per frame, F is the number of frames, and P is the number of points. We are unable to go into more details of the method but refer to [15].

2.4 Stitching Subsequences

Subsequence computation is performed with a few frames overlap between consecutive subsequences. The points that are visible in two overlapping subsequences

24

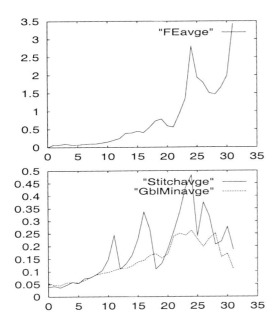

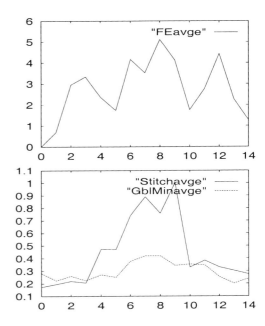

Figure 4: Average reprojection error distribution over the 32 frames of *Garden* sequence for the three processing stages. **Top**: **FE** errors. **Bottom**: Solid line is **Stitch** errors and dotted line is **GblMin** errors.

Figure 5: Average reprojection error distribution over the 15 frames of *Dorm* sequence for the three processing stages. **Top**: **FE** errors. **Bottom**: Solid line is **Stitch** errors and dotted line is **GblMin** errors.

are used to represent both the subsequences in a common coordinate system. A common 3D point has two different representations in two subsequences: $\mathbf{P}_{s1}$ and $\mathbf{P}_{s2}$ but the same image frame is used in the two subsequences. Then the image projection can be written in two ways in Eqn. 1, one with the camera matrix with the pose $\{R_1, \mathbf{T}_1\}$ and the other with the pose $\{R_2, \mathbf{T}_2\}$. Therefore, there is a similarity transformation corresponding to $\{s, R, \mathbf{T}\}$ such that the two 3D representations of each point and the two camera representations of the same frame are identical. That is, from Eqn. 1, $M_{s1} = M_{s2}S^{-1}$, and $[\mathbf{P}_{s1}\ 1]^T = S\,[\mathbf{P}_{s2}\ 1]^T$. The unknown similarity transformation S is computed by minimizing an image based error measure:

$$\sum_n d^2(\mathbf{p}_n, \Pi(M_{s1}S\,[\mathbf{P}_{s2,n}\ 1]^T)) + d^2(\mathbf{p}_n, \Pi(M_{s2}S^{-1}\,[\mathbf{P}_{s1,n}\ 1]^T))$$

2.5 Global Adjustment

The stitching of subsequences allows the representation of poses and the 3D points in a single coordinate system. However, point tracks that are common across more than one subsequence provide constraints for further global adjustment of the 3D parameters. In the final step, bundle block adjustment as described for subsequence computation in Section 2.3, is applied to the complete set of frames and 3D points. For computational efficiency, this adjustment can be applied in small sets of arbitrary frames or can be applied to the complete set. The interesting aspect of the representation here is that any combination of internal parameters, pose parameters or 3D points can be adjusted while maintaining a global representation.

3 Pose Estimation Results

The performance of our approach is shown both quantitatively and in terms of the visual stability of 3D object insertion. Three video sequences that are representative of three different types of motions that may be used in 3D model acquisition and in video post-production type applications. The first has motion mostly in the view direction (T_z) with rotations and change of motion, the second is a fixation type motion, and the third is almost pure translatory motion parallel (T_y) to the image plane simulating an aerial platform. Note that good results have been shown primarily for fixation type sequences in the literature [9, 4, 18] whereas we obtain end-to-end results for all three.

For quantitative results, we computed the reprojection errors (the difference in pixels in the location of a projected 3D point and its measured image location) for each frame at various stages of processing. The processing stages are abbreviated as: (i) **FE** : the stage, called the *FrontEnd*, at which the pairwise camera estimates with respect to a reference in a sub-sequence are combined using a common scale factor, (ii) **Stitch** : where the overlapping sub-sequences are stitched together and represented in a consistent coordinate system using similarity transformations, and (iii) **GblMin** : the final global adjustment that combines all the 3D point and pose estimates in one optimization. For each of the three video sequences, we will show plots of the *average* errors for each frame over all the visible points in that frame.

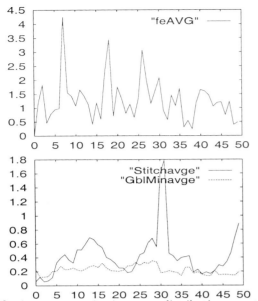

Figure 6: Average reprojection error distribution over the 50 frames of *Terrian* sequence for the three processing stages. **Top**: **FE** errors. **Bottom**: Solid line is **Stitch** errors and dotted line is **GblMin** errors.

Garden Sequence: T_z motion with rotation and change of motion.

The first sequence, called *garden*, is a sequence of 97 frames that are sub-sampled by 3 to create a sequence of length 32. The size of each frame is 1024×768. The camera FOV is about 45°. The camera moves first mostly along the view axis and then turns sideways. Four frames of the sequence are shown in Fig. 1. (There are some markers put on the fence but that is the way we were handed the sequence; we did not use any of the markers for tracking.) It is to be emphasized that there are not many visually distinctive features in this sequence. Using the auto-correlation and flow-based tracker, a total of 757 points were tracked over the 32 frames with the number per frame ranging from 200 to 30. After outlier removal, finally, 732 points were used for the global adjustment. The distribution of errors at various stages of processing are shown in Fig. 4. The highlight of the results is the progressive reduction in re-projection errors. Consider the mean error in each frame. The maximum value of the mean error per frame reduces from 3.429 pixels after **FE** to 0.482 pixels after **Stitch**, and further to 0.262 after **GblMin**. Likewise, the mean of the mean errors per frame goes down from 0.646 pixels to 0.188 pixels and finally to 0.139 pixels.

Dorm Sequence: Fixation type motion

The second sequence is a 15-frame sequence of a Princeton University dormitory that was captured as 640×480 frames using a Sony digital camera. The camera FOV was about 50°. Three frames of the sequence are shown in Fig. 2. The camera was moved around the building to keep it in view and hence this is

an example of a fixation like sequence, the one considered ideal for model acquisition. A total of 431 points were tracked with points in each frame ranging from 81 to 241. Again, the maximum value of the mean error per frame reduces from 4.125 pixels after **FE** to 1.003 after **Stitch**, and further to 0.420 pixels after **GblMin**. Likewise, the mean of the mean errors per frame goes down from 2.008 pixels to 0.450 pixels and finally to 0.297 pixels. The distribution of errors at various stages of processing are shown in Fig. 5. The pose estimates drawn as camera coordinates in *VRML* are shown in Fig. 7.

Figure 7: Poses for the *dorm* sequence shown in *VRML*. Blue is the view axis (Z), red and green are the X and Y axes.

Terrain Sequence: Primarily T_y motion

The third sequence is a 50-frame sequence of a terrain model captured using a camcorder attached to a gantry to simulate aerial motion. The camera was zoomed in so that the FOV was only about 10°. Unfortunately, the gantry set up is only able to move the camera but not give any pose information. The video was digitized to 320×240 frames and was temporally sampled by 4. Therefore, the effective length of the sequence is 200 frames. Four frames of the sequence are shown in Fig. 3. The distribution of errors at various stages of processing are shown in Fig. 6. As before, a maximum error averaged over all the 50 frame of 5.563 pixels after **FE** reduces to 1.788 pixels after **Stitch** and to 0.353 pixels after **GblMin**. The mean of the average frame errors for the three stages processing are 1.661, 0.427 and 0.220 pixels respectively. The distribution of errors over all the frames at various stages of processing are shown in Fig. 6. It is to be emphasized that with as small an FOV as 10°, the results of pose and 3D estimation are quite good. It is well known that two-frame estimates in such an imaging situation suffer from an ambiguity between rotations and the depth scale (and translation), the bas-relief ambiguity [1]. However, the effective field of view is enhanced by our multi-frame tracking and local-to-global optimization strategy, and hence reliable results are obtained even in this situation. Further analytical work to understand the role of local-to-global in this scenario is being carried out.

The maximum, average and median errors for the

average errors over all the frames for the three sequences are summarized in Table 1.

To emphasize that not only are the 3D poses computed, but the tracked set of points are also reconstructed well, Fig. 11 shows a VRML generated view of the texture mapped model of the *dorm* and the top view of the point cloud that is reconstructed. The texture mapping is done by defining triangles over one reference image. Note that we are not attempting a complete 3D reconstruction but want to show that both 3D poses and points are recovered well.

Figure 8: Poses for the *Garden* sequence. Blue is the view axis (Z), red and green are the X and Y axes.

4 3D Match Move

Accurate and stable pose estimation is important for the application of 3D match move in which synthetic objects are inserted into real images and their viewpoints are mimicked according to the real camera's pose and internal parameters. Now we show examples of 3D match move using the pose estimation technique presented in the earlier part of the paper.

The 3D pose and point cloud estimates for the sampled sequence of 32 frames of the *Garden* sequence were used to compute the poses of all the intermediate frames by keeping the 3D point cloud fixed. Subsequently, synthetic 3D objects were inserted. Fig. 9 shows three original frames of the *Garden* sequence in which some synthetic objects have been inserted. The object was inserted in the 3D coordinates of the scene points created by the algorithm and in the coordinate system of one camera, the first camera frame. A plane fit was obtained for a set of 3D points within a window specified around the location of the desired insertion in the first frame. One face of the object was placed on the plane with the dominant normal along the normal of the plane. Once the synthetic object was placed with respect to the real surface in the reference frame, all other views of the object were created using OpenInventor and the computed camera transformations.

A similar insertion for the *Dorm* sequence is shown in Fig. 10. It is to be emphasized that in both the data sets, the placement of the synthetics has been done with

respect to one frame only and that too with respect to the 3D surface computed by the algorithm. Therefore, there is minimal interaction demanded of the user. It is to be emphasized that both in the still image displays as well as in the videos, no drift or jitter in the objects in any of the frames is noticeable. This is a qualitative visual validation of the stability of pose and 3D structure computation of the algorithm developed.

Table 1: Summary of *max* and *avg* errors over all the frames after the three stages of processing for three sequences.

Seq. Name	No. of Frames	Measure	FE	Stitch	GblMin
Garden	32	MAX	3.429	0.482	0.262
		AVG	0.646	0.188	0.139
		MED	0.365	0.175	0.130
Dorm	15	MAX	4.125	1.003	0.420
		AVG	2.151	0.450	0.297
		MED	2.147	0.330	0.270
Terrain	50	MAX	5.563	1.788	0.353
		AVG	1.695	0.427	0.220
		MED	1.656	0.384	0.212

5 Conclusions

A number of issues need to be further explored. First, stability of pose estimation over much longer videos, for instance, tens of seconds to a few minutes, needs to be further established. Also, assessing the quality of the estimation for higher resolution data, for example at film resolutions, is extremely important for the techniques to be viable in the real world. Occlusions between synthetic and reals has been ignored in this work but is obviously important.

References

[1] G. Adiv. Inherent ambiguities in recovering 3D information from a noisy flow field. *IEEE PAMI*, 11(5):477–489, 1989.

[2] J. R. Bergen et al. Hierarchical model–based motion estimation. In *Proc. 2nd European Conference on Computer Vision*, pages 237–252, 1992.

[3] O. Faugeras and R. Keriven. Complete dense stereovision using level set methods. In *ECCV*, pages 379–393, 1998.

[4] Andrew W. Fitzgibbon and Andrew Zisserman. Automatic camera recovery for closed or open image sequences. In *ECCV*, Frieburg, Germany, 1998.

[5] K. J. Hanna and Neil E. Okamoto. Combining stereo and motion analysis for direct estimation of scene structure. In *Proc. Intl. Conf. on Computer Vision*, pages 357–365, 1993.

[6] R. Hartley and P.Sturm. Triangulation. In *Proc. DARPA Image Understanding Workshop*, pages 957–966, 1994.

[7] R. I. Hartley. Estimation of relative camera positions for uncalibrated cameras. In *Proc. 2nd European Conference on Computer Vision*, pages 579–587, 1992.

[8] R. I. Hartley. Euclidean reconstruction from uncalibrated views. In *Joint European-US Workshop on Applications of Invariance in Computer Vision*, 1993.

[9] Reinhard Koch, Marc Pollefeys, and Luc Van Gool. Multi viewpoint stereo from uncalibrated video sequences. In *ECCV*, Frieburg, Germany, 1998.

Figure 9: Three frames of the *Garden* sequence with synthetic 3D flamingoes inserted. The 3D placement was done only in one frame, and all others were generated through rendering using the automatically computed poses.

Figure 10: Three frames of the *dorm* sequence with two synthetic 3D pyramids inserted.The 3D placement was done only in one frame, and all others were generated through rendering using the automatically computed poses.

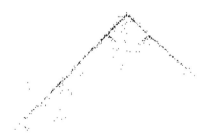

Figure 11: VRML snapshots of texture mapped 3D triangles defined over the reconstructed 3D points, and the top view of the 3D point cloud.

[10] K. N. Kutulakos and J. R. Vallino. Calibration-free augmented reality. *IEEE TVCG*, 4:1–20, 1998.

[11] B.D. Lucas and T. Kanade. An iterative image registration technique with an application to stereo vision. In *Image Understanding Workshop*, pages 121–130, 1981.

[12] Princeton Video Image. http://www.pvimage.com.

[13] Harpreet S. Sawhney, Steve Hsu, and R. Kumar. Robust video mosaicing through topology inference and local to global alignment. In *ECCV*, pages 103–119, 1998.

[14] Steven M. Seitz and Charles R. Dyer. Photorealistic scene reconstruction by voxel coloring. In *Proc. Computer Vision and Pattern Recognition Conference*, pages 1067–1073, 1997.

[15] C. C. Slama. *Manual of Photogrammetry*. Amer. Soc. of Photogrammetry, Falls Church, VA, 1980.

[16] Andrei State et al. Superior augmented reality registration by integrating landmark tracking and magnetic tracking. In *SIGGRAPH*, pages 429–438, 1996.

[17] R. Szeliski and H. Shum. Creating full view panoramic image mosaics and environment maps. In *Proc. of SIGGRAPH*, pages 251–258, 1997.

[18] C. Tomasi and T. Kanade. Shape and motion from image streams under orthography: A factorization method. *International Journal of Computer Vision*, 9(2):137–154, 1992.

[19] P. H. S. Torr and A. Zisserman. Robust parameterization and computation of the trifocal tensor. *Image and Vision Computing*, 24:271–300, 1997.

[20] W.H.Press, B.P.Flannery, S.A.Teukolsky, and W.T.Vetterling. *Numerical Recipes in C*. Cambridge University Press, 1986.

[21] Z. Zhang et al. A robust technique for matching two uncalibrated images through the recovery of the unknown epipolar geometry. *Artificial Intelligence*, 78:87–119, 1995.

Calibrating a Multi-Camera System for 3D Modelling

Charles Wiles and Allan Davison

Computer Vision Group, Canon Research Centre Europe
Guildford, Surrey, UK, GU2 5YJ

Abstract

This paper describes a simple and novel way for calibrating the position and internal camera parameters of a camera viewing a scene with no prior knowledge of the camera being necessary. Only two views of a simple planar grid of spots are used to accurately determine the relative position of each camera in a multiple camera system. A multiple camera system is necessary for modelling dynamic objects (such as people). When the shape of the object is continually changing a large number of images must be taken simultaneously. The multiple camera system is also an important research tool allowing surface generation algorithms to be investigated under known accuracy in the camera positions. We have evaluated our algorithm's performance using simulations to determine the limits on the accuracy of our system and have demonstrated the performance in practice by producing 3D models from a four camera system.

1 Introduction

1.1 Motivation

Computing 3D models of a scene from multiple images observing the scene involves two key steps. First the relative position of the camera to the object being modelled must be determined for each image (*camera solving*), second the 3D structure of the object is computed by intersecting the coloured rays observed in the pixels of each image (*surface generation*).

Various methods exist for computing camera positions. When a single hand-held camera is used to record multiple images of a static scene from different positions the position of the camera can be computed by matching distinguishable *features* on surfaces in the scene between views and employing a *structure from motion* algorithm. Although such an approach works well when the features are accurately matched it can fail when few distinguishable features are visible in the scene. Moreover, such a system fails when the scene is dynamic, containing for example a human being.

To avoid feature matching problems prior to camera

solving the camera positions can be either computed by observing a *calibration* object in the scene or *measured* directly using an alternative device. To model an arbitrary dynamic scene it is necessary to record multiple images from different views at the same instant in time; hence multiple cameras are necessary.

For these reasons, we have explored the use of a calibrated multi-camera 3D modelling system. Not only does such a system allow dynamic objects with few distinguishable features to be modelled, but it provides a valuable research tool for investigating surface generation algorithms, since the accuracy of the camera positions can be independently established. Indeed, the accuracy, coverage and robustness plus the choice of algorithm for surface generation depends greatly on the accuracy of the camera positions determined.

1.2 Issues

There are several important research issues concerning calibrated multiple camera systems:

- Prior knowledge of camera intrinsic parameters

- Ease of production of calibration object

- Ease of calibration process

- The number of images that need to be taken (few images are suitable for still cameras, whereas many images can be used for video cameras).

- Range of camera positions from which the camera can view the calibration object well enough to be calibrated

- Accuracy of calibration

- Accuracy of matching image data to the calibration model

There is clearly a trade off between such factors since the most accurate calibration process would likely require a complicated calibration object and process. However, one of the key aims of our work has been to find the simplest object and process possible to give us a predefined accuracy in calibration.

We define *object space* to be the limit on 3D space within which the object to be modelled is assumed to lie (for a human being this might be a 2x2x2m cube of space). Our goal in calibrating the camera positions is to recover them such that any point within object space projects to within 1 pixel of its true projection in the image. By achieving a *maximum projection error* of less than 1 pixel we limit the range of search for agreeing texture in image co-ordinates to 1 pixel from predicted positions during surface generation.

Unfortunately this does not give us a clear measure of the accuracy of the surface generated when correct matches are found between images under surface generation. It does, however, guarantee that the surface of the model will project to within 1 pixel of its true observed position in the original images. We argue that this measure of accuracy on camera position is more important when the goal is to generate a model that is *photo-consistent* with the original images.

1.3 Background

The most accurate calibration object and process would be to have a known 3D point observed in the image for every point in object space and to compute the transfer equation that projects these points into the observed image co-ordinates.

In practice the act of projection is assumed to be a simple parameterised type called a *camera model*. If the parameters (known as the *intrinsic parameters*) of this projection are known then only three world-to-image point matches are required in order to fix the six degrees of freedom in the unknown orientation and location of the camera (known as the camera *extrinsic parameters*)[1]. If the intrinsic parameters are not known then, depending on the nature of the calibration object, it is possible to compute these parameters at the same time as the extrinsic parameters from a larger number of matches[2]. In practice noise in the image measurements of the observed points is inevitable and many matches are required so that the maximum likelihood solution can be found by least squares.

In our work we have assumed that the camera model may radially distort the image during projection and that the intrinsic parameters are unknown in advance. Given this starting point the problem is significantly more complicated than computing just

---

[1]In fact, two or four different solutions are obtained under projective imaging conditions and exactly two different solutions are obtained under affine imaging conditions.

[2]For example for the perspective camera model, the four intrinsic and six extrinsic parameters can be computed from five 2D-3D point matches when the points are non-coplanar.

the extrinsic parameters when the intrinsic parameters are known in advance. One reason for taking this approach is that although manufacturers often provide accurate values for the *focal length* of their cameras, the position of the *principal point* often varies greatly and is unknown. Accurate knowledge of the principal point is vital for computing accurate camera position from coplanar world points (see [4]).

There are several methods that have been used to calibrate both intrinsic and extrinsic parameters of a camera. Perhaps the simplest method is to take a single image of a planar calibration grid of known structure. This method was pioneered by Tsai [8]. Although this method is simple, it is only capable of completely calibrating both the intrinsic and extrinsic parameters of the camera if the imaging process exhibits significant radial distortion. If there is little or no radial distortion, the position of the principal point in the image cannot be determined independently from the height of the camera above the calibration plane, and hence calibration fails to provide a complete answer.

In order to calibrate the intrinsic parameters from a planar grid when no radial distortion occurs, multiple images of the grid must be taken. This is the method used by Kanade et al [2] to calibrate their multi-camera rig for dynamic 3D modelling of people. First a planar grid is moved randomly around in front of each video camera to calibrate the intrinsic parameters of the camera, second each camera's position is computed relative to a grid of spots on the floor. The method gives good accuracy of calibration, but uses many images for each camera to carry out the calibration. Our method, presented later, adapts this method to work with just two images from a still camera.

The problem with a single image of a planar grid is solved if an accurate three-dimensional calibration grid is manufactured. Typically an "L" shaped grid is used which has a pattern of black squares on a white background on each of the two flat surfaces. Such calibration grids allow reasonably accurate calibration of the camera to be performed from a single image of the grid and this method has been used extensively for calibrating stereo-camera rigs [1]. The main draw back of such an approach is that accurate manufacturing of the calibration grid is necessary and this is both awkward and expensive. Moreover, such a system does not scale well to large environments and the calibration object must be carefully orientated so that all cameras see a "good" view of the object.

An alternative method is to use a planar calibration

grid, but to move it through space in a *known* motion. Either a robot arm or a stepper motor is used to move the grid. By moving the grid in known steps and taking an image after each step, the whole object space can be swept out providing a wealth of matches. Such systems can provide very accurate camera calibration, and although the planar calibration object can be easily made the main drawback is in the expense of the robot arm or stepper motor and in the lack of scalability of the system. Since many images should be recorded for each camera, it is suitable for calibrating video cameras, but is not an ideal method for calibrating still cameras.

More recently "magic wands" [10] have been used to calibrate multiple camera systems. The magic wand approach is to move a single point (or pair of points one at each end of a wand) by hand randomly around in space. Typically the scene is darkened and a point light source is used. The actual algorithm for computing the extrinsic parameters is similar to self-calibration [6] from an unknown object (or structure from motion, if the intrinsic parameters of the cameras are known), but is simpler since the matching problem is trivially solved between images. This method scales well and is inexpensive. It is an excellent method for calibrating multiple video camera rigs, but due to only one point appearing in each image it is not suitable for the calibration of multiple still camera rigs. A further consideration for the magic wand approach are that if a full self-calibration technique is used with a wand with a single point certain camera configurations must be avoided (for example, the cameras must not all lie in the same plane). However if a wand with points at both ends is used then the ambiguity in the Euclidean reconstruction is removed and full self-calibration is possible.

2 Accurate calibration from a planar grid

Our method for calibrating a multiple still camera rig uses a simple planar calibration grid of regularly spaced black circles on a white background. Such a grid is trivial to manufacture (by for example printing on a standard home printer).

The challenge then is to accurately calibrate the position and intrinsic parameters of a number of cameras that observe the grid. Our method stems from the observation that all the intrinsic parameters of a camera can be accurately determined from a small number of images of a planar grid taken with the camera at different positions without needing to know any of the camera positions in advance. Indeed if the camera positions are chosen reasonably carefully, the calibration

can be done from just two images. If one of these images was recorded with the camera in its final position in the multi-camera system then accurate calibration of the multi-camera system can be achieved with just two images from each camera. Additional images provide greater accuracy to the calibration.

The process for calibration is as follows:

1. Take an image of the calibration grid with the camera rotated by roughly 90° about the viewing direction and with a different tilt from the final orientation in the multiple camera rig.

2. Put the camera in its final position in the multiple camera rig and secure in place. Take a second image of the calibration grid.

With the camera in its final position, the calibration grid can be removed and objects to be modelled placed within the space observed by the multi-camera rig.

2.1 Calibrating from a single image

Tsai[7] pioneered the process of calibrating a camera from a planar grid. Tsai's camera model projecting world point $\mathbf{X} = (X, Y, Z)^\top$ to image point $\mathbf{x} = (x, y)^\top$ is defined by the set of equations:

$$\mathbf{x} = 1/(1 + \kappa_1 R_n^2) \begin{bmatrix} \xi f & 0 \\ 0 & f \end{bmatrix} \mathbf{x}_n + \mathbf{x}_0,$$

where

$$R_n^2 = x_n^2 + y_n^2$$

and

$$\mathbf{x}_n = \frac{1}{Z_c} \begin{pmatrix} X_c \\ Y_c \end{pmatrix}, \quad \text{where} \quad \mathbf{X}_c = \mathbf{R}\mathbf{X} + \mathbf{t}.$$

$\mathbf{R}$ and $\mathbf{t}$ are the 3x3 rotation matrix and translation vector representing the position of the camera, and aspect ratio ξ, focal length f, principal point $\mathbf{x}_0 = (x_0, y_0)^\top$ and first order radial distortion coefficient κ_1 are the five intrinsic parameters of the camera. If the aspect ratio is known and the distortion coefficient is significant then all the intrinsic and extrinsic parameters can be computed from five or more world-to-image point matches. As well as the radial distortion coefficient being significant it is important that the projection of the grid in the image exhibits significant perspective effects. Hence the camera cannot be calibrated if it is far from the calibration grid or if the viewing direction is close to perpendicular to the plane of the grid. In practice this is easy to avoid.

However, when the first order radial distortion coefficient is zero then the imaging equation reduces to the standard, linear perspective camera model which has 10 parameters (4 intrinsic + 6 extrinsic). In this case the planar grid to image mapping is completely defined by a linear planar homography containing 8 independent parameters. Hence even when the aspect ratio is known the total number of parameters to be estimated in order to calibrate the camera is still 9 (3 unknown intrinsic + 6 extrinsic) which is clearly not possible.

In the rest of this section we argue that the position of the principal point in the direction parallel to the plane of the calibration grid is determined uniquely, but that the component perpendicular to the plane of the calibration grid cannot be determined independently from the rest of the camera parameters. Indeed we gain an insight into this problem by considering the case when the x-axis of the camera is known to be parallel to the XZ-plane of the world so that the roll of the camera is zero with respect to this plane.

The equation for the perspective camera model in homogeneous co-ordinates is

$$\begin{pmatrix} \mathbf{x} \\ 1 \end{pmatrix} = \mathbf{P} \begin{pmatrix} \mathbf{X} \\ 1 \end{pmatrix},$$

where

$$\mathbf{P} = \mathbf{K} \begin{bmatrix} \mathbf{R} & \mathbf{t} \end{bmatrix} \quad , \quad \mathbf{K} = \begin{bmatrix} \xi f & 0 & x_0 \\ 0 & f & y_0 \\ 0 & 0 & 1 \end{bmatrix}$$

and equality is only defined up to an arbitrary scale factor. In this case of no camera roll we can rewrite the perspective camera model in terms of only the pitch, α, and yaw, β, of the rotation matrix:

$$\mathbf{R} = \begin{bmatrix} 1 & 0 & 0 \\ 0 & c_\alpha & s_\alpha \\ 0 & -s_\alpha & c_\alpha \end{bmatrix} \begin{bmatrix} c_\beta & 0 & s_\beta \\ 0 & 1 & 0 \\ -s_\beta & 0 & c_\beta \end{bmatrix}$$

where c_θ and s_θ are the cosine and sine of angle θ respectively.

If we further note that under calibration from a planar grid, the world points on the grid are considered to be in the world plane $Y = 0$, then we can remove the second column of the rotation matrix, $\mathbf{R_2}$, and the Y structure co-ordinate from the equation for projection. Thus we can rewrite the equation for projection in terms of the 3x3 planar homography $\mathbf{H}$,

$$\begin{pmatrix} x \\ 1 \end{pmatrix} = \mathbf{K} \begin{bmatrix} \mathbf{R_1} & \mathbf{R_3} & \mathbf{t} \end{bmatrix} \begin{pmatrix} X \\ Z \\ 1 \end{pmatrix} = \mathbf{H} \begin{pmatrix} X \\ Z \\ 1 \end{pmatrix}.$$

Simplification of $\mathbf{H}$ leads to,

$$\begin{pmatrix} \mathbf{x} \\ 1 \end{pmatrix} = \begin{bmatrix} f_g c_\beta - x_0 s_\beta & f_g s_\beta - x_0 c_\beta & t'_x \\ y_h(-s_\beta) & y_h c_\beta & t'_y \\ -s_\beta & c_\beta & t'_z \end{bmatrix} \begin{bmatrix} X \\ Z \\ 1 \end{bmatrix}$$

where $f_g = \xi f / c_\alpha$, $y_h = y_0 + f \tan(\alpha)$ is the *horizon* of the calibration plane in the image and $\mathbf{t}'$ contains some reparameterisation of the vector $\mathbf{t}$.

The important observation is that only seven independent parameters can be observed in $\mathbf{H}$ despite having nine elements in the matrix (we have fixed the scale using the bottom row of the matrix). Having fixed the roll angle to be zero and assuming that the aspect ratio is known, we would like to compute all eight unknown perspective camera parameters (3 unknown intrinsic + 5 unknown extrinsic). However of these only the yaw, and the x co-ordinate of the principal point can actually be computed.

Although the argument above is valid for only special case of zero camera roll we have observed empirically that for arbitrary camera orientation, the roll, yaw and component of the principal point parallel to the plane of the calibration grid can indeed be observed from a single image for arbitrary camera roll. The pitch, focal length, translation vector and component of the principal point perpendicular to the plane of the calibration grid cannot be observed.

2.2 Calibrating from a pair of images

The observation that for a perspective camera one component of the principal point can be determined from a single view, but that the perpendicular component cannot, leads directly to a simple method for calibration from two views of the calibration grid.

With two views of the grid, assuming the intrinsic parameters of the camera are unchanged between views, there are 16 independent parameters determined by the two homographies and there are 16 parameters to be estimated in the two cameras (4 fixed intrinsic parameters and 2 sets of 6 extrinsic parameters). With known aspect ratio there are only 15 parameters to be estimated, but in either case there are theoretically enough equations to determine all the unknown parameters.

The key question then is, given that there are theoretically enough equations to solve for all the unknowns, *under what conditions is this possible?*

Recall that in the special case of zero roll we are left with two equations in the unobservable parameters:

$$f_g = \xi f / c_\alpha \quad \text{and} \quad y_h = y_0 + f \tan(\alpha).$$

We will consider that we require only to determine the four remaining unknown parameters in these two equations having solved from a single view for the other intrinsic and extrinsic parameters. Each additional view of the calibration grid gives one more set of these two equations but introduces one additional unknown (the pitch of the camera in the new view).

For the case of known aspect ratio and two views then the equations above give four equations in four remaining unknown parameters. Examination of the equations above show that as long as the pitch of the camera changes between the two views of the calibration grid, then the camera can be fully calibrated. Our first conjecture is then

- if the aspect ratio is known in advance then as long as the pitch of the camera changes between two views then the camera can be fully calibrated from two views of a planar calibration grid.

For the case of unknown aspect ratio there are four equations in five remaining unknown parameters and four equations. Hence calibration cannot be computed from two views of the grid. Our second conjecture is then

- if the aspect ratio is not known in advance and there is no change in the roll angle between the two views then the camera cannot be fully calibrated from two views of a planar calibration grid.

However, for the case of when there *is* a change in the roll angle of the camera between two views then an interesting simplification occurs, since the principal point becomes uniquely determined. This is because each view fixes the principal point to lie on a specific line in the image, the line being perpendicular to the plane of the calibration grid. If the roll angle changes these lines will not be parallel and hence will intersect at the location of the principal point. Algebraically, y_0 is effectively known in the above equations reducing the number of unknown parameters from five to four. So our third and final conjecture is that:

- if the aspect ratio is not known in advance and there is both a change in the roll angle and a change in the tilt angle between the two views then the camera can be fully calibrated from two views of a planar calibration grid.

Hence in order for the camera intrinsic parameters to be determined fully from two views there must be relative roll (with respect to the plane of the calibration grid) between the positions of the two cameras. Indeed ideally the relative roll should be 90°.

2.3 Accurate feature location

Our approach to matching the calibration object to image data has been to extract the location in the image of point features of known location on the calibration object forming world-to-image point matches. These co-ordinates are then fed into an algorithm for calibrating the camera parameters. A key goal of our

work is to determine the accuracy in feature location needed in order to guarantee a maximum projection error in object space of less than 1 pixel.

More accurate calibration may well be achievable by following the initial "calibration from matches" stage with an iterative "template matching" stage. This second stage would aim to globally minimise the difference between a template of the calibration object and the raw image data. We have not yet implemented such a stage and hence our evaluation for calibration performance is based on the first stage only and may be improved by template matching.

3 Results
3.1 Synthetic data

In order to validate experimentally our prediction that only one component of the principal point can be localised accurately under calibration from a single plane we performed the following experiment using synthetic data.

First the intrinsic parameters and position of a camera were computed fully automatically from a typical view of a calibration grid with the aspect ratio known in advance. The roll of the camera with respect to the plane of the calibration grid was zero and the camera was tilted so that the centre of the grid projects to the centre of the image. The grid fills the unit square and is centred at (0.5, 0.5, 0.0) in the world. The camera is at (0.7, -1.0, 1.0). Since the roll of the camera is zero we expect that the x co-ordinate of the principal point will be accurately located and the y co-ordinate less accurately located getting progressively worse as the amount of radial distortion decreases.

We then repeated each experiment using two views of the grid, one view as in the single view experiment and a second view rotated by 90° about the viewing direction. The aspect ratio was calculated being assumed unknown in advance.

In both cases the maximum projection error within the unit cube of space above the calibration grid was measured as well as the projection error of the point in the centre of the unit cube.

Tsai's freely available code was used to carry out the minimisation with slight modification to enable minimisation of the two view case. Note that for the case of a single view with no radial distortion the minimisation is clearly under-constrained and hence it would be wise reparameterise the solution. However we found this to be unnecessary since the full minimisation reliably and rapidly converged on a solution in which the observable parameters were accurately recovered.

The process for solving for the two view case was as follows:

1. Solve for each view separately using Tsai's single view approach (using a fixed prior estimate for the aspect ratio).

2. Determine the roll of the camera.

3. From the principal point for each view extract the component parallel to the calibration plane and combine into an initial estimate of the principal point.

4. Solve again for each view separately keeping this principal point fixed.

5. Average the intrinsic parameters from each view and use these and the two sets of extrinsic parameters as an initial estimate for a final full two view minimisation.

These experiments were then repeated with non zero roll. The solution computed from a single view accurately recovers the roll of the camera in the extrinsic parameters and hence it is straight forward to extract and combine the components of the principal point parallel to the calibration plane as a precursor to full two view minimisation.

3.1.1 Effect of varying RMS image noise on errors

In this experiment the performance of the full calibration method was measured as the noise in the image co-ordinates of the matches was varied. The experiment was repeated with varying amounts of radial distortion. The full results can be found in [9].

The main observations for calibration from a single view were:

- The estimation of the y co-ordinate of the principal point, y_0, is computed less accurately than the x co-ordinate of the principal point, x_0.

- The accuracy of the y co-ordinate of the principal point decreases as the amount of radial distortion decreases.

- The accuracy of the x co-ordinate of the principal point is independent of the amount of radial distortion.

- The maximum projection error of the unit cube sitting directly above the calibration grid is highly correlated with the error in y_0.

- The maximum projection error occurs for points farthest from the calibration grid and is approximately ten times greater than the error in the projection of the centre point of the unit cube.

In essence when the roll of the camera is zero the estimation of the y_0 intrinsic parameter from a single view is poorly constrained. This leads to errors in projection of 3D points and the further away from the plane of the calibration grid the 3D point being projected is the greater the error in the projection. However, the x_0 intrinsic parameter is well constrained.

The main observations from two views were:

- The error in the y_0 intrinsic parameter was recovered to the same level of accuracy as the x_0 parameter irrespective of the amount of radial distortion

- The maximum projection error for both views was greatly reduced compared with the projection error observed from a single view with the same value of image noise. This difference became more marked the lower the amount of radial distortion.

- With no radial distortion in order to calibrate the camera so that the maximum projection error is guaranteed to be less than one pixel the RMS image noise in the image co-ordinates of features must be less than 0.05 pixels.

- With no radial distortion in order to guarantees the centre projection error to be less than one pixel the image noise must be less than 0.25 pixels.

3.2 Real data

Two experiments were carried out, both using the same set of four off-the-shelf PowershotA5 cameras. In the first experiment, the cameras were positioned around a toy dinosaur to demonstrate small scale modelling, whereas in the second experiment the cameras were positioned in a room so that a person could be modelled.

3.3 Toy dinosaur

A calibration grid printed onto a sheet of A4 paper was placed on a stand. Each of the four cameras were held in a portrait orientation and a photograph of the grid taken as shown in the first column of Figure 2.

Then the cameras were set up as shown in Figure 1 with each camera in a landscape orientation. Three cameras were positioned roughly by hand so that they were about 20cm above the plane of the calibration grid and evenly spaced in a circle about the grid. The fourth camera was positioned so that it was roughly

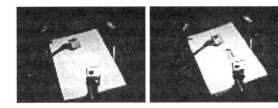

Figure 1: Camera configuration. a) calibration grid imaged, b) toy dinosaur imaged.

above the centre of the grid looking down. A second photograph of the grid was taken with each camera as shown in the second column of Figure 2.

The grid was then removed and in keeping with the indomitable spirit of the academic computer vision community a toy dinosaur placed in the space where the grid had been. A photograph of the dinosaur was taken with each camera.

The three images from each camera were then downloaded to a PC. Two frame calibration as described above was carried out for each camera in turn to calculate its intrinsic parameters and position with respect to the calibration grid in the second image.

Finally the dinosaur images were segmented from the background using a blue screening technique and a voxel carve [7] applied to work out an outer bound on the space occupied by the toy dinosaur (though a better approach would be to use voxel *coloring* [3]). The resulting voxelisation was transformed using a marching cubes algorithm into a faceted VRML model for display. Figure 3 shows the resulting model viewed from the same direction as given in one of the images. The accuracy of the camera calibration is demonstrated by a plausible reconstruction of the toy dinosaur. In particular the tail of the dinosaur is well reconstructed.

3.3.1 Person

A calibration grid was made by sticking together 63 sheets of A4 paper each with a single black circle printed on each. The 7x9 grid occupied a space approximately 1.5m x 1.5m.

First a photograph of the grid was taken with each of three cameras. Then the cameras were placed in their final position roughly evenly spaced through 180° and a second photograph was taken of the calibration grid as shown in the first row of Figure 4. Finally the calibration grid was removed from the scene and a photograph of Aimy taken with each camera.

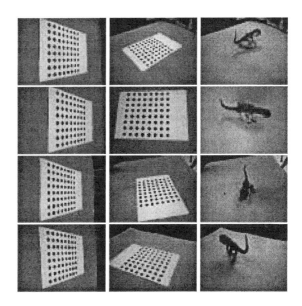

Figure 2: Toy dinosaur images. First column: photographs taken of grid with each camera in portrait orientation (roll angle approximately 90°). Second column: photographs taken with camera in final position in landscape orientation (roll angle approximately 0°). Third column: photographs of toy dinosaur with cameras in final position.

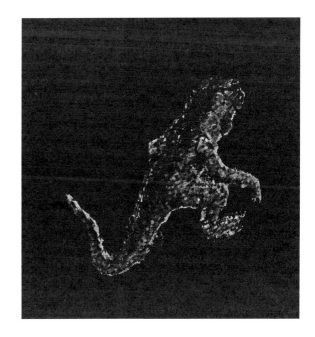

Figure 3: View of the 3D model computed from the toy dinosaur images

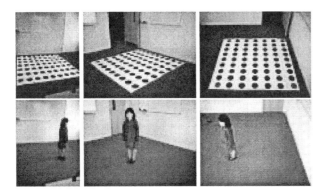

Figure 4: Aimy images. First row: photographs of the calibration grid with cameras in final position (the first camera was placed in portrait orientation whereas the other two were placed in landscape orientation). Second row: photographs of Aimy.

A faceted model was reconstructed as before as shown in Figure 5. The accuracy of the camera calibration is demonstrated by a plausible reconstruction of Aimy.

4   Conclusion

We have shown that accurate camera calibration can be achieved with a simple two views of a plane technique and have demonstrated its practicality by using it to calibrate a multi-camera system for modelling real objects of varying size. Future work will focus on improved techniques for surface generation.

Acknowledgments

The authors would like to thank Ricahrd Taylor, Jane Haslam, Adam Baumberg, Alex Lyons, Simon Rowe and Mike Taylor for their sofware implementations and Philip McLauchlan for helpful discussions.

References

[1] O. Faugeras. *Three-Dimensional Computer Vision.* The MIT Press. 1993.

[2] T. Kanade, P.J. Narayanan, and P.W. Rander. "Virtualized Reality: Constructing virtual worlds from real scenes". *IEEE Multimedia*, 4(1), May 1997.

[3] K.N. Kutulakos and S.M. Seitz. "A theory of shape by space carving". *University of Rochester Computer Sciences Technical Reort 692*, May 1998.

[4] R.K. Lenz, and R.Y. Tsai. "Techniques for calibration of the scale factor and image centre for high accuracy 3D machine vision metrology". *Proc. IEEE Int. Conf. Robotics and Automation*, Raleigh, NC, 68-75, March 1987.

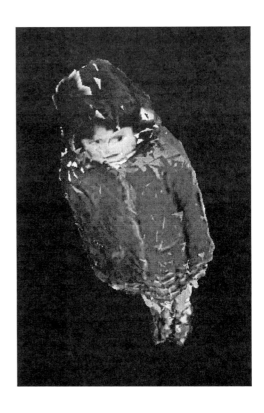

Figure 5: View of the 3D model computed for Aimy

[5] W. Niem and J. Wingbermulhle. "Automatic reconstruction using a mobile monoscopic camera". *Proc. International Conference on Recent Advances in 3D Imaging and Modelling.* Ottawa, Canada, 12-15 May 1997.

[6] M. Pollefeys, R Koch and L Van Gool. "Self-calibration and metric reconstruction in spite of varying and unknown intrinsic camera parameters". *Proc. International Conference on Computer Vision*, Bombay, India, January 1998.

[7] R. Szeliski. "Rapid octree construction from image sequences". *CVGIP: Image Understanding*, 58(1):23-32, July 1993.

[8] R.Y. Tsai. "A versatile camera calibration technique for high accuracy 3D machine vision metrology using off-the-shelf TV cameras and lenses". *IEEE Journal of Robotics and Automation*, RA-3(4):323-344, 1987.

[9] C. Wiles. "Calibrating and 3D modelling with a multi-camera system". *Canon Technical Report CRE-TR-98-043*, 14 December 1998.

[10] Oxford Metrics. http://www.oxfordmetrics.co.uk/

Gauge Invariance in Projective 3D Reconstruction

Philip F. McLauchlan,

School of Electrical Engineering, Information Technology and Mathematics,
University of Surrey, Guildford GU2 5XH, UK
Email P.McLauchlan@ee.surrey.ac.uk

Abstract

Bundle adjustment is a standard photogrammetric technique for optimizing the 3D reconstruction of a scene from multiple images. There is an inherent gauge (coordinate frame) ambiguity in 3D reconstruction that can seriously affect the convergence of bundle adjustment algorithms. We address this issue and show that a simple pre-conditioning step removes the effect of the choice of coordinate frame, and together with a set of enforced constraints on the reconstruction, achieves along with this invariance greatly increased convergence speed over existing methods. The new approach applies to all the well-known 3D reconstruction models: projective, affine and Euclidean. In this paper we develop the idea for projective reconstruction.

The normalization stage partially removes the gauge freedom, reducing the coordinate frame choice from a general 3D homography to an orthogonal transformation; then constraints are incorporated in the bundle adjustment iterations that enforce the normalisation condition to first order. In the projective case the approach relies on a currently unproven matrix conjecture, which we nevertheless strongly believe to be correct, based on extensive experimental evidence.

1 Introduction

We first summarize the results to be derived in detail later. Given a 3D projective reconstruction of a scene represented by k projective camera matrices (3×4) $P_{(j)}$, $j = 1, \ldots, k$, describing the transformation from scene to image, and n projective 3D points $\mathbf{X}_i$, $i = 1, \ldots, n$, it is well known that there is a space of equivalent reconstructions of the same scene given the same image data, related to each other by 3D projective linear transformations (homographies). Thus given another equivalent reconstruction $P'_{(j)}$, $\mathbf{X}'_i$, the two must be related by

$$P'_{(j)} = \mu_{(j)} P_{(j)} H, \quad \mathbf{X}'_i = \mu_i H^{-1} \mathbf{X}_i$$

for some 4×4 invertible matrix H, where the $\mu_{(j)}$ and μ_i are scale factors. Our first result is that it is possible to normalize a projective reconstruction so that the matrix factor relating the normalized reconstruction to another normalized reconstruction is reduced from a general 4×4 matrix to an *orthogonal* 4×4 matrix U:

$$P'_{\text{norm}(j)} = P_{\text{norm}(j)} U, \quad \mathbf{X}'_{i\,\text{norm}} = U^{-1} \mathbf{X}_{i\,\text{norm}}$$

where $U^\top U = U U^\top = I$. The normalization also removes the scale factors $\mu_{(j)}$, μ_i, so the normalization specifies an appropriate scaling for the projective quantities. The normalization procedure is independent of the order of the images. This result makes it possible to build an optimization algorithm for projective 3D reconstruction whose performance is invariant to the choice of projective coordinate frame, by pre-normalizing the latest reconstruction before each iteration.

The second advance presented here is a way to constrain the reconstruction inside a bundle adjustment algorithm, so that the coordinate frame ambiguity in adjusted solutions is eliminated, again in a manner invariant to the coordinate frame and the ordering of the images. This is achieved by enforcing the normalisation conditions to first order inside each bundle adjustment iteration.

The combination of the two ideas above improves upon the various devices used to eliminate the redundant degrees of freedom inherent in 3D reconstruction (see below). We will present experimental evidence of greatly increased convergence speed of bundle adjustment, when our procedures are followed. The normalization and constraint procedure generalizes easily to the cases of affine and Euclidean 3D reconstruction, although details are omitted because of lack of space.

2 Previous Work

The Tomasi & Kanade factorization algorithm [18] is a statistically optimal and gauge invariant algorithm for reconstructing 3D points under affine projection. Invariant 3D projective reconstruction algorithms for point features,

37

also based on factorization using the SVD, have been described by Sturm & Triggs [17] and Berthilsson et al. [2]. In fact Berthilsson et al. go further than this; their algorithm is designed to be invariant to a 2D affine transformation of image coordinates, as well as 3D projective transformation of space, although this feature seems of dubious value since statistical properties of image feature error are at most Euclidean invariant. There are drawbacks with these factorization approaches:–

- They require complete observations. Every feature must be observed in every image. Our scheme, although presented in that way for simplicity, trivially generalizes without any change to the invariance properties, simply by leaving relevant terms out of the formulæ presented below.

- They only work for point features. Factorization has been extended to the case of lines in [15], but at the expense of losing the optimality property. Bundle adjustment can be seamlessly generalized to other features such as lines, as we demonstrated in [11, 12].

- The projective algorithms do not minimize geometric error on the image plane, and so are not as accurate as bundle adjustment. Berthillson et al. report a 50% larger reprojection (geometric) error over the level of added noise.

Nevertheless these algorithms are good ways to generate starting points for a projective bundle adjustment algorithm, and indeed Heyden makes the point in [8] that the combination of factorization methods and bundle adjustment would make an attractive combination of robustness and accuracy. For instance, one could apply a factorization algorithm to a subset of features with complete data, and use the motion parameters thus computed to compute the rest of the structure. In this way it would be easy to develop a coordinate-system-independent starting point for optimization.

Triggs [19] discusses solutions to the problem of gauge freedoms in the optimization, which occur frequently in vision. He describes the main two approaches, *gauge fixing conditions*, which break the degeneracy by the introduction of artificial constraints, such as imposing a canonical frame (see below), and *free gauge methods*, such as free bundle adjustment, which allow the gauge to drift, but control it through the use of numerical damping methods such as regularization. Ours is a gauge fixing scheme, and we employ artificial constraints to fix the gauge, which are introduced by the "method of weighting" [4, page 586], i.e. as weighted residual errors minimized along with the geometric error. In subsequent work we will investigate the direct method for solving constrained least-squares problems described in [4], which would avoid the arbitrary choice of weights.

In photogrammetric bundle adjustment, the standard solution is the use of known control points to define and fix

the gauge. Where control points are not available, a suggested alternative is to select a number of observed 3D points, and constrain the solution to keep the adjusted points close to their original position by regularization [9]. Clearly the result of this procedure depends on the choice of selected points.

The *canonical frame* [10, 13, 1] is a gauge fixing method that fixes the values of certain elements of specific camera matrices. In the simplest approach, one would fix the first projection matrix to the canonical form $P(1) = (I_{3\times3}|\mathbf{0})$ and impose four constraints on another $P(j)$, for instance setting a row to (0 0 0 1). In this way the coordinate frame for the reconstruction may be fixed to any desired camera coordinate frame. The problem with this procedure is that the results depend on the choice of which projection matrices to fix; while achieving gauge invariance, we have introduced a new problem of varying results according to the ordering of the images. By contrast, our methods are invariant to the coordinate frame *and* image ordering.

Our normalization procedure has similarities with the pre-conditioning of image data known to improve the performance of the linear 8-point fundamental matrix algorithm [7].

3 Projective Bundle Adjustment

3D projective reconstruction is simple to describe, and it seems sensible to start with projective reconstruction to illustrate the problems involved. We are here only concerned with bundle adjustment; that is optimising an existing approximate reconstruction, so we shall assume that feature correspondence has been successfully achieved, and an initial reconstruction computed. These two steps can be integrated using robust statistical methods; see [3]. Alternative methods of computing projective reconstructions from any number of images are described in [17, 2].

We shall take the simplest case of reconstructing a set of n 3D scene points $\mathbf{X}_i$, $i = 1, \ldots, n$ from a set of k images of them, $j = 1, \ldots, k$. The projection model is

$$\mathbf{p}_i(j) = \mu_i(j)P(j)\mathbf{X}_i + \text{noise}, \qquad (1)$$

where

$\mathbf{p}_i(j) = (x_i(j)\ y_i(j)\ 1)^\top$ is the position of the image feature corresponding to the i'th feature as seen in the j'th image, in homogeneous coordinates,

$\mu_i(j)$ is a scale factor,

$P(j)$ is a 3×4 projection matrix, defining the projection from the scene to the j image frame in projective terms, and

$\mathbf{X}_i$ is the i'th projective point.

To simplify the notation, we shall assume that the image data is complete, in the sense that every point i has a projection in every image j. Our methods are in no sense dependent on this assumption, although we must assume that there are "enough" features in every image (in this case 6) in order to solve for the P's.

We now consider the application of the standard Levenberg-Marquardt algorithm to this problem [14]. The parameters to be estimated are those of the projection matrices $P_{(j)}$ and structure $\mathbf{X}_i$. We first briefly describe the general algorithm, and then apply it to our problem of projective 3D reconstruction.

3.1 The Levenberg-Marquardt algorithm

The Levenberg-Marquardt algorithm [14] is a general minimization algorithm for the case when derivatives of the objective function can be computed, when necessary numerically. It dynamically mixes Gauss-Newton and gradient-descent techniques. Let the unknown parameters be represented by the vector $\mathbf{x}$, and let noisy measurements of $\mathbf{x}$ be made:

$$\mathbf{z}_{(j)} = \mathbf{h}_{(j)}(\mathbf{x}) + \mathbf{w}_{(j)}, \quad j = 1, \dots, k \quad (2)$$

where $\mathbf{h}_{(j)}(.)$ is a measurement function and $\mathbf{w}_{(j)}$ is zero-mean noise with covariance $R_{(j)}$. Since we are describing an iterative minimization algorithm, we shall assume that we have already obtained an estimate $\mathbf{x}^-$ of $\mathbf{x}$. Then the maximum likelihood solution for a new estimate $\mathbf{x}^+$ minimizes

$$J(\mathbf{x}^+) = \sum_{j=1}^{k} (\mathbf{z}_{(j)} - \mathbf{h}_{(j)}(\mathbf{x}^+))^\top R_{(j)}^{-1} (\mathbf{z}_{(j)} - \mathbf{h}_{(j)}(\mathbf{x}^+)).$$

$$(3)$$

We form a quadratic approximation to $J(.)$ around $\mathbf{x}^-$, and locate the minimum of this approximation to $J(.)$ to obtain a new estimate $\mathbf{x}^+$. The second-order extrapolation of $J(.)$ is obtained using only the value of $J(.)$ and its derivatives at $\mathbf{x}^-$; second derivative terms are ignored. We can write a single L-M update as

$$\mathbf{x}^+ = \mathbf{x}^- + A^{-1} \left(\sum_{j=1}^{k} H_{(j)}^\top R_{(j)}^{-1} \boldsymbol{\nu}_{(j)} \right), \quad (4)$$

where:–

- $\boldsymbol{\nu}_{(j)} = \mathbf{z}_{(j)} - \mathbf{h}_{(j)}(\mathbf{x}^-)$, the innovation vectors.

- $H_{(j)} = \partial \mathbf{h}_{(j)} / \partial \mathbf{x}$, the Jacobian matrices, with the derivatives evaluated at $\mathbf{x}^-$.

- $A = \sum_{j=1}^{k} H_{(j)}^\top R_{(j)}^{-1} H_{(j)}$, the symmetric positive semi-definite matrix, which may be identified as the information (inverse covariance) matrix for the new estimate $\mathbf{x}^+$.

The update (4) may be repeated, substituting the new $\mathbf{x}^+$ as $\mathbf{x}^-$, and improving the estimate until convergence is achieved according to some criterion, such as a small change to the parameter vector $\mathbf{x}$, or a limit on the number of iterations. The version of the Levenberg-Marquardt algorithm given in [14] modifies this updating procedure by scaling the diagonal elements of A by a factor $1 + \lambda$ before inverting it. The value of λ is adjusted using a control scheme.

3.2 Applying Levenberg-Marquardt to projective reconstruction

To apply the above procedure we first stack all the unknown parameters into a single parameter vector $\mathbf{x}$. To do this, we write

$$P_{(j)} = \begin{pmatrix} \mathbf{P}_{1(j)}^\top \\ \mathbf{P}_{2(j)}^\top \\ \mathbf{P}_{3(j)}^\top \end{pmatrix}$$

and then we can build the parameter vector as

$$\mathbf{x} = \begin{pmatrix} \mathbf{X}_1 \\ \vdots \\ \mathbf{X}_n \\ \mathbf{P}_{1(1)} \\ \mathbf{P}_{2(1)} \\ \mathbf{P}_{3(1)} \\ \vdots \\ \vdots \\ \mathbf{P}_{1(k)} \\ \mathbf{P}_{2(k)} \\ \mathbf{P}_{3(k)} \end{pmatrix} = \begin{pmatrix} \mathbf{x}_{l\,1} \\ \vdots \\ \mathbf{x}_{l\,n} \\ \mathbf{x}_{d(1)} \\ \vdots \\ \mathbf{x}_{d(k)} \end{pmatrix} = \begin{pmatrix} \mathbf{x}_l \\ \mathbf{x}_d \end{pmatrix}$$

where the structure $\mathbf{X}_i$ and motion $P_{(j)}$ parameters are bundled separately into vectors $\mathbf{x}_l$ and $\mathbf{x}_d$. Applying Levenberg-Marquardt to this system with the set of image measurements (1), we first write the measurements in the form of (2) by eliminating the scale factors $\mu_{i(j)}$, obtaining

$$\begin{aligned} \mathbf{z}_i(j) &= \begin{pmatrix} x_i(j) \\ y_i(j) \end{pmatrix} \\ &= \begin{pmatrix} \frac{\mathbf{P}_{1(j)}^\top \mathbf{X}_i}{\mathbf{P}_{3(j)}^\top \mathbf{X}_i} \\ \frac{\mathbf{P}_{2(j)}^\top \mathbf{X}_i}{\mathbf{P}_{3(j)}^\top \mathbf{X}_i} \end{pmatrix} + \text{noise} \\ &= \mathbf{h}(\mathbf{x}_{l\,i}, \mathbf{x}_{d(j)}) + \mathbf{w}_i(j) \end{aligned} \quad (5)$$

Note that the measurement function $\mathbf{h}(.)$ is here the same for every measurement. We then obtain the following update rule:

$$\begin{pmatrix} \mathbf{x}_l^+ \\ \mathbf{x}_d^+ \end{pmatrix} = \begin{pmatrix} \mathbf{x}_l^- \\ \mathbf{x}_d^- \end{pmatrix} + \begin{pmatrix} A_{ll} & A_{ld} \\ A_{ld}^\top & A_{dd} \end{pmatrix}^{-1} \begin{pmatrix} \mathbf{a}_l \\ \mathbf{a}_d \end{pmatrix} \quad (6)$$

as a partitioned form of the L-M update rule (4), where

$$\mathbf{x}_l^{+/-} = \begin{pmatrix} \mathbf{x}_{l\,1}^{+/-} \\ \mathbf{x}_{l\,2}^{+/-} \\ \vdots \\ \mathbf{x}_{l\,n}^{+/-} \end{pmatrix}, \quad \mathbf{x}_d^{+/-} = \begin{pmatrix} \mathbf{x}_d^{+/-}(1) \\ \mathbf{x}_d^{+/-}(2) \\ \vdots \\ \mathbf{x}_d^{+/-}(k) \end{pmatrix},$$

$$A_{ll} = \begin{pmatrix} A_{ll\,1} & 0 & \ldots & 0 \\ 0 & A_{ll\,2} & \cdot & \vdots \\ \vdots & \cdot & \cdot & \vdots \\ 0 & \ldots & 0 & A_{ll\,n} \end{pmatrix}, \quad (7)$$

$$A_{ld} = \begin{pmatrix} A_{ld\,1(1)} & A_{ld\,1(2)} & \ldots & A_{ld\,1(k)} \\ A_{ld\,2(1)} & \cdot & \cdot & A_{ld\,2(k)} \\ \vdots & \cdot & \cdot & \vdots \\ A_{ld\,n(1)} & \ldots & \ldots & A_{ld\,n(k)} \end{pmatrix},$$

$$A_{dd} = \begin{pmatrix} A_{dd(1)} & 0 & \ldots & 0 \\ 0 & A_{dd(2)} & \cdot & \vdots \\ \vdots & \cdot & \cdot & \vdots \\ 0 & \ldots & 0 & A_{dd(k)} \end{pmatrix}, \quad (8)$$

$$\mathbf{a}_l = \begin{pmatrix} \mathbf{a}_{l\,1} \\ \mathbf{a}_{l\,2} \\ \vdots \\ \mathbf{a}_{l\,n} \end{pmatrix}, \quad \mathbf{a}_d = \begin{pmatrix} \mathbf{a}_{d(1)} \\ \mathbf{a}_{l(2)} \\ \vdots \\ \mathbf{a}_{l(k)} \end{pmatrix},$$

the matrix blocks are defined as

$$A_{ll\,i} = \sum_{j=1}^{k} H_{l\,i(j)}^{\top} R_{i(j)}^{-1} H_{l\,i(j)}.$$

$$A_{dd(j)} = \sum_{i=1}^{n} H_{d\,i(j)}^{\top} R_{i(j)}^{-1} H_{d\,i(j)}.$$

$$A_{ld\,i(j)} = A_{dl\,i(j)}^{\top} = H_{l\,i(j)}^{\top} R_{i(j)}^{-1} H_{d\,i(j)}.$$

The partitioning of $\mathbf{a}$ is

$$\mathbf{a}_{l\,i} = \sum_{j=1}^{k} H_{l\,(j)}^{\top} R_{i(j)}^{-1} \boldsymbol{\nu}_{i(j)},$$

$$\mathbf{a}_{d(j)} = \sum_{i=1}^{n} H_{d\,(j)}^{\top} R_{i(j)}^{-1} \boldsymbol{\nu}_{i(j)},$$

and the other terms are

$H_{l\,i(j)} = \partial \mathbf{h}/\partial \mathbf{x}_l$ and $H_{l\,i(j)} = \partial \mathbf{h}/\partial \mathbf{x}_d$, both evaluated at $\mathbf{x}_{l\,i}^{-}$, $\mathbf{x}_{d}^{-}(j)$).

$\boldsymbol{\nu}_{i(j)} = \mathbf{z}_{i(j)} - \mathbf{h}(\mathbf{x}_{l\,i}^{-}, \mathbf{x}_{d}^{-}(j))$. This measures the image-plane error between the actual feature position $\mathbf{z}_{i(j)}$ and the projected 3D feature position $\mathbf{h}(\mathbf{x}_{l\,i}^{-}, \mathbf{x}_{d}^{-}(j))$.

The sparsity of the matrices A_{ll} and A_{dd} results from the fact that each measurement $\mathbf{z}_{i(j)}$ involves only a single structure vector $\mathbf{x}_{l\,i}$ and motion parameter vector $\mathbf{x}_{d(j)}$. The sparse structure may be used to accelerate the computations, and to this end our implementation [12] uses the recursive partitioning algorithm [16]. Now we shall investigate the existence, uniqueness and invariance properties of the updated solution vectors $\mathbf{x}_l^{+}$, $\mathbf{x}_d^{+}$ under a change of projective coordinate frame.

3.3 Changing the coordinate frame

We consider now an alternative, equivalent representation $P'_{(j)}$, $\mathbf{X}'_i$ of the same scene given the same image data. This corresponds to choosing a different coordinate frame to represent the scene points $\mathbf{X}'_i$. To be equivalent, the two representations must be related by a linear projective transformation which we shall represent as a 4×4 matrix F:

$$P'_{(j)} = P_{(j)}F, \quad \mathbf{X}'_i = F^{-1}\mathbf{X}_i, \quad (9)$$

In terms of the parameter vectors, we have

$$\mathbf{x}'_{l\,i} = F^{-1}\mathbf{x}_{l\,i}, \quad \mathbf{x}'_{d(j)} = \begin{pmatrix} F^{\top} & 0 & 0 \\ 0 & F^{\top} & 0 \\ 0 & 0 & F^{\top} \end{pmatrix} \quad (10)$$

The matrix F cancels in the projection equations (1), (5), so any such alternative reconstruction cannot be distinguished from any other using the image data (this is what it means to say that a projective reconstruction is only "up to" a 3D projective transformation). Our criterion for invariance is that if any two alternative projective reconstructions are related by a coordinate change F before an update, they should be related by the same F *after* the update. To achieve this we first have to normalize the reconstructions so that F is converted to an orthogonal matrix. So now we ask: what effect does the matrix F have on the update equation (6)?

We can write down the modified Jacobian terms for the transformed problem, and show how they relate to the original $H_{l\,i(j)}$ and $H_{d\,i(j)}$. We have by the chain rule

$$H'_{l\,i(j)} = \frac{\partial \mathbf{h}}{\partial \mathbf{x}'_l} = H_{l\,i(j)} \frac{\partial \mathbf{x}_l}{\partial \mathbf{x}'_l} = H_{l\,i(j)}F \quad (11)$$

In a similar way we can obtain the result

$$H'_{d\,i(j)} = H_{d\,i(j)} \begin{pmatrix} F^{-\top} & 0 & 0 \\ 0 & F^{-\top} & 0 \\ 0 & 0 & F^{-\top} \end{pmatrix} \quad (12)$$

Now if we construct a diagonal block matrix F_D of size $n + 3k$ blocks from n blocks of $F^{-\top}$ and $3k$ blocks of F, we will have

$$\begin{aligned} \mathbf{x}'^{+} &= \mathbf{x}'^{-} + A'^{-1}\mathbf{a}' \\ &= \mathbf{x}'^{-} + \left(F_D^{\top} A F_D\right)^{-1} F_D^{\top}\mathbf{a} \quad (13) \end{aligned}$$

If we were able to use the matrix inverse directly, we would immediately have gauge invariance, because then we would have

$$\begin{aligned} \mathbf{x}'^{+} &= \mathbf{x}'^{-} + F_D^{\top} A^{-1}\mathbf{a} \\ &= F_D^{\top}(\mathbf{x}^{-} + A^{-1}\mathbf{a}), \quad (14) \end{aligned}$$

as one would expect to maintain the same transformation F_D between the parameter vector estimates for $\mathbf{x}$ and $\mathbf{x}'$ before and after the adjustment. However the existence of a space of equivalent solutions related by 3D projective transformations implies that the matrix A in (6) has 15 null vectors (the elements of F up to scale). Given that every projection matrix $P_{(j)}$ and 3D point $\mathbf{X}_i$ has a scale freedom, the total size of the null-space of A is $k + n + 15$. These freedoms will be dealt with below using artificial constraints. The first stage in our algorithm is to normalize the projective matrices and 3D points so that the possible space of coordinate frames is reduced from the space of projective linear transformations to the space of *orthogonal* transformations, so that F (and hence F_D) becomes

40

orthogonal. The benefits of this normalization will become clear, after we describe the procedure. First we state an important although as yet unproven result.

4 Conjecture concerning normalization

Let B_i, $i = 1, \ldots, n$ be rectangular matrices all having the same dimensions. For instance they could be projective camera matrices (3×4) or (transposed) projective 3D points (1×4). Assume first that the matrix formed by stacking the B_i vertically has full column rank, or alternatively that $\sum_{i=1}^{n} B_i^\top B_i$ is full-rank. Also assume that all the rows of each matrix are non-zero. If the B_i represent row-vectors, we have found that we require one more B_i than required purely for rank purposes, i.e. n must be at least three for 2-vectors, and at least four for 3-vectors. Then our conjecture states that there exists an invertible lower triangular matrix L and a scalar ξ such that

$$\sum_{i=1}^{n} \frac{L^{-1} B_i^\top B_i L^{-\top}}{\|B_i L^{-\top}\|_F^2} = \xi I. \tag{15}$$

where I is identity and $\|.\|_F$ signifies the Frobenius matrix norm. L is uniquely defined up to scale, for the given set of matrices B_i. The value of ξ is $n/\text{SIZE}(L)$, where $\text{SIZE}(.)$ returns the size of a (square) matrix. The experimental evidence for this conjecture is that the algorithm formed by iterating the equivalent formula

$$S = \sum_{i=1}^{n} \frac{\xi^{-1} B_i^\top B_i}{\text{trace}(B_i S^{-1} B_i^\top)}. \tag{16}$$

for many different sets B_i, evaluating the right-hand side for an estimate of S, and reading off the new estimate of S on the left, etc., appears always to converge. Then L can be recovered from the Cholesky factorisation $S = LL^\top$. The two formulæ (15) and (16) are equivalent because for any matrix B, symmetric positive definite $S = LL^\top$ and lower-triangular L,

$$\text{trace}(BSB^\top) = \|BL\|_F^2,$$

This follows from the easily verifiable fact that for any matrix A, $\text{trace}(AA^\top) = \|A\|_F^2$, on setting $A = BL$.

Also, for a given set B_i, different starting values S_0 of S produce the same solution for S (up to scale). However there are some degenerate cases, and the domain of convergence is not yet accurately characterised.

Assuming that the above conjecture is true, we can show that given a different set C_i of matrices related to the B_i by a linear transformation F along with arbitrary scaling factors λ_i, the above result allows us to normalize the B_i and C_i to within an orthogonal transformation of each other.

4.1 Lemma

Given matrices B_i obeying the above assumptions, and C_i related to B_i as $C_i = \lambda_i B_i F$, for scale factors $\lambda_i \neq 0$ and invertible square matrix F, and given symmetric

matrices S_B and S_C computed by the above procedure (16), one can construct matrices B_i' and C_i' with the property that $C_i' = B_i' U$ for some orthogonal matrix U. The B_i' and C_i' are related to the original B_i and C_i by a linear transformation and scaling.

Proof: Assuming that the above conjecture is correct, we first of all show that $S_C = \mu F^\top S_B F$ for some positive scalar μ. To do this we only need to check that substituting $\mu F^\top S_B F$ for S and C_i for B_i satisfies equation (16) for arbitrary μ, since S_C is (conjectured to be) unique up to scale.

Now we substitute C_i for B_i and $\mu F^\top S_B F$ for S_B on the RHS of (16) and expand, obtaining

$$\begin{aligned} S_C &= \sum_{i=1}^{n} \frac{\xi^{-1} C_i^\top C_i}{\text{trace}(C_i (\mu F^\top S_B F)^{-1} C_i^\top)} \\ &= \sum_{i=1}^{n} \frac{\xi^{-1} \lambda_i^2 F^\top B_i^\top B_i F}{\text{trace}(\lambda_i^2 \mu^{-1} B_i F F^{-1} S_B^{-1} F^{-\top} F^\top B_i^\top)} \\ &= \mu F^\top \sum_{i=1}^{n} \frac{\xi^{-1} B_i^\top B_i}{\text{trace}(B_i S_B^{-1} B_i^\top)} F \\ &= \mu F^\top S_B F \end{aligned}$$

as expected. Now we can construct the normalized matrices B_i' and C_i' as

$$B_i' = \frac{1}{\|B_i L_B^{-\top}\|_F} B_i L_B^{-\top}, \quad C_i' = \frac{1}{\|C_i L_C^{-\top}\|_F} C_i L_C^{-\top}, \tag{17}$$

where L_B and L_C are the Cholesky factors of S_B and S_C. It is easy to show that given the relationship $S_C = \mu F^\top S_B F$, L_B and L_C are related by

$$L_C = \sqrt{\mu} F^\top L_B U$$

where U is an orthogonal matrix: $UU^\top = U^\top U = I$. Thus we have

$$\begin{aligned} C_i' &= \frac{\lambda_i \sqrt{\mu} B_i F F^{-1} L_B^{-\top} U}{\|\lambda_i \sqrt{\mu} B_i F F^{-1} L_B^{-\top} U\|_F} \\ &= \frac{\|B_i L_B^{-\top}\|_F B_i' L_B^\top L_B^{-\top} U}{\|B_i L_B^{-\top}\|_F \|B_i' L_B^\top L_B^{-\top} U\|_F} \\ &= \frac{1}{\|B_i' U\|_F} B_i' U \\ &= B_i' U, \end{aligned}$$

the last following because the Frobenius norm is invariant to orthogonal transformations and $\|B_i'\|_F = 1$. So we have transformed and scaled the B_i and C_i to within an orthogonal transformation of each other. As well as having unit Frobenius norm, the normalized matrices B_i' and C_i' have the property

$$\sum_{i=1}^{n} B_i'^\top B_i' = \sum_{i=1}^{n} C_i'^\top C_i' = \frac{n}{\text{SIZE}(S)} I \tag{18}$$

where I is the identity matrix. We can gain some intuition into the benefits of the above transformation from B_i to B_i', by noting that it optimally "spreads out" the B_i in the space of matrices. Interpreting the matrix $\sum_{i=1}^{n} B_i^\top B_i$ as the moment of inertia B_i, we can see that the transformation is such that $\sum_{i=1}^{n} B_i'^\top B_i' = k^{-1}I$, i.e. the moment of inertia is proportional to identity. This means that the B_i' are spread evenly around the origin. For example, if the B_i consist of four 3D row vectors, the B_i' will be points on a unit tetrahedron, and the C_i' then constitute a rotated (and possibly reflected) copy of this tetrahedron.

We apply the normalisation to the projective camera matrices $P_{(j)}$, so that after normalisation they satisfy

$$\sum_{j=1}^{k} P_{(j)}^\top P_{(j)} = \frac{k}{4}I, \qquad (19)$$

and apply the inverse of the normalising transformation to the 3D structure vectors $\mathbf{X}_i$.

5   Constraining the Reconstruction

The camera matrix normalization procedure takes us part of the way towards cordinate-system invariant bundle adjustment. We still have the problem of the null-space in the information matrix A in the update (6). We propose to eliminate the null-space by introducing extra constraints into the update. These constraints are chosen to enforce the normalisation, but more constraints are needed and these are chosen for their invariance properties. Firstly, to remove the $n + k$ degrees of freedom corresponding to the scale factors for the projective points and camera matrices we introduce extra "virtual" observations into the Levenberg-Marquardt update:

$$\|\mathbf{X}_i\|^2 = \|P_{(j)}\|_F^2 = 1, \quad i = 1, \ldots, n, \ j = 1, \ldots, k$$

Note that the constraint on $P_{(j)}$ is imposed by the normalization procedure, while the $\mathbf{X}_i$ should be rescaled to unit norm after the normalization. To incorporate these constraints into L-M we introduce $n + k$ virtual measurements with the measurement functions

$$\mathbf{h}_l(\mathbf{x}_{l\,i}) = (\|\mathbf{x}_{l\,i}\|^2), \quad \mathbf{h}_d(\mathbf{x}_{d(j)}) = (\|\mathbf{x}_{d(j)}\|^2),$$

for $i = 1, \ldots, n$ and $j = 1, \ldots, k$. The elements of the measurement "vectors" $\mathbf{z}_{l\,i}$ and $\mathbf{z}_{d(j)}$ are set to 1. The error covariances $R_{l\,i}$, $R_{d(j)}$ (inverse weights) are arbitrary, but in practice may be set to widely different values with negligible effect on the results. Because each such measurement involves only a single parameter vector $\mathbf{x}_{l\,i}$ or $\mathbf{x}_{d(j)}$, only diagonal blocks of the block matrices A_{ll} and A_{dd} are incremented ($\mathbf{a}_l$ and $\mathbf{a}_d$ are not affected because the innovations ν of the virtual measurements are zero), and the sparseness of A is not affected. To show that these measurements have the correct covariance properties, we only need to show that

the modified A they produce obeys the same transformation rule

$$A \to F_D^\top A F_D \qquad (20)$$

under the change of coordinates F_D, as in equation (13), because then the properties of the matrix inverse (which we may use now that we are removing the redundancy in the system) guarantee identical results, as demonstrated by equation (14). This implies that the Jacobians of our virtual measurement functions should obey the same transformation rules (11) and (12) as the image measurements. i.e.

$$\frac{\partial \mathbf{h}_l}{\partial \mathbf{x}_{l\,i}'} = \frac{\partial \mathbf{h}_l}{\partial \mathbf{x}_{l\,i}}F, \quad \frac{\partial \mathbf{h}_d}{\partial \mathbf{x}_{d(j)}'} = \frac{\partial \mathbf{h}_d}{\partial \mathbf{x}_{d(j)}} \begin{pmatrix} F & 0 & 0 \\ 0 & F & 0 \\ 0 & 0 & F \end{pmatrix}^{-\top}.$$

These relationships are easily verified given that

$$\frac{\partial \mathbf{h}_l}{\partial \mathbf{x}_{l\,i}} = 2\mathbf{x}_{l\,i}^\top, \quad \frac{\partial \mathbf{h}_d}{\partial \mathbf{x}_{d(j)}} = 2\mathbf{x}_{d(j)}^\top.$$

It remains to remove the 15 degrees of freedom associated with the coordinate frame. We can do this partially by enforcing the normalisation (19), but this leaves six undetermined degrees of freedom, because the normalisation is invariant to 4×4 orthogonal transformations, which are defined by six "angles". These last degrees of freedom are removed by suppressing changes that merely apply the same orthogonal transformation to all the $P_{(j)}$'s. This can be done by forcing the off-diagonal elements of the anti-symmetric matrix

$$\sum_{j=1}^{k} (P^+{}_{(j)}^\top P^-{}_{(j)} - P^-{}_{(j)}^\top P^+{}_{(j)})$$

to be zero. This can be demonstrated by computing the Jacobians of these elements with respect to $P^+{}_{(j)}$ and showing that they correspond to the coefficients of small rotation angles between the $P^-{}_{(j)}$ and $P^+{}_{(j)}$.

Thus we construct a measurement function $\mathbf{h}(.)$ from the ten independent elements of the symmetric matrix $\sum_{j=1}^{k} P^+{}_{(j)}^\top P^+{}_{(j)}$ together with the six below-diagonal elements of $\sum_{j=1}^{k} (P^+{}_{(j)}^\top P^-{}_{(j)} - P^-{}_{(j)}^\top P^+{}_{(j)})$. The elements of the corresponding measurement vector $\mathbf{z}$ are set to $\frac{k}{4}$ for the diagonal elements of $\sum_{j=1}^{k} P^+{}_{(j)}^\top P^+{}_{(j)}$ and zeroes for the other elements. The innovation vector $\nu = \mathbf{z} - \mathbf{h}(\mathbf{x}^-)$ will again be zero, because all the constraints are satisfied by the projection matrices $P^-{}_{(j)}$. It may be verified that the Jacobians of this measurement satisfies the covariance condition (12). The measurement is again assigned a covariance, and then the measurement Jacobians are incorporated in the Levenberg-Marquardt update by incrementing A_{dd} in (6) in the same way as for the image measurements.

Because this last measurement involves all the dynamic state vectors, it spoils the sparse structure of A_{dd} in (8), but this has no effect on the performance of the bundle adjustment so long as the structure blocks A_{ll} are eliminated first in the partitioned elimination scheme [16, 5, 12][1].

A subtle point is that although we started out with 15 redundant degrees of freedom to remove, we have imposed 16 constraints in our virtual measurement. However we have verified experimentally that the 16 virtual measurements taken together have an (unknown) dependence, so that in fact they only impose the desired 15 constraints.

6 Levenberg-Marquardt scaling

A final problem is that the usual version of the Levenberg-Marquardt algorithm rescales only the diagonal elements of the information matrix A prior to inverting it. This again raises invariance issues, since under orthogonal transformations such a rescaled matrix would fail our invariance criterion (20). However since the orthogonal transformations operate on the individual blocks of A, modifying L-M to rescaling the diagonal *blocks* $A_{ll\ i}$ and $A_{dd(j)}$ of A, rather than just the diagonal elements of those blocks, solves this problem and recovers invariance.

7 Summary of Algorithm

We can now summarize the procedure detailed previously for applying invariant projective bundle adjustment. We are given initial camera matrices $P(j)$ and structure vectors $\mathbf{X}_i$, where $j = 1, \ldots, k$ and $i = 1, \ldots, n$. We are also provided with image measurements $\mathbf{z}_i(j)$, and a starting value for the Levenberg-Marquardt scaling parameter λ. The procedure is as follows:

Repeat Levenberg-Marquardt iterations:–

1. Apply the projection matrix normalization to the latest estimated projection matrices $P(j)$ and structure vectors $\mathbf{X}_i$, linearly transforming and rescaling them to $P'(j)$ and $\mathbf{X}'_i$ having the properties

$$\|\mathbf{X}'_i\|^2 = \|P'(j)\|_F^2 = 1, \quad \sum_{j=1}^{k} P'(j)^\top P'(j) = \frac{k}{4} I$$

The normalization is applied to the projection matrices, while the structure vectors are transformed by the inverse of the normalizing transformation and scaled to unit length.

2. Set the prior parameter vectors for this iteration to

$$\mathbf{x}_{l\ i}^- = \mathbf{X}'_i, \quad \mathbf{x}_{d(j)}^- = \left(\mathbf{P}'_1(j)^\top \quad \mathbf{P}'_2(j)^\top \quad \mathbf{P}'_3(j)^\top \right)^\top$$

3. Construct the $n + k + 16$ "virtual measurements" to impose constraints on the L-M adjustment.

4. Construct the information matrix A and vector $\mathbf{a}$ from the image measurements and virtual measurements.

[1]If there are more images k than features n, it is advantageous to eliminate the motion blocks A_{dd} first. In this case an equivalent normalization and virtual measurement scheme based on the structure vectors $\mathbf{X}_i$ may be used.

5. Scale the diagonal blocks $A_{ll\ i}$ and $A_{dd(j)}$ of A by the factor $1 + \lambda$.

6. Update the parameter vectors to $\mathbf{x}_{l\ i}^+$ and $\mathbf{x}_d^+(j)$ according to the update formula (6), using recursive partitioning to speed up the computation [16, 12].

7. Read off the new reconstruction $P(j)$, $\mathbf{X}_i$ from $\mathbf{x}_{l\ i}^+$ and $\mathbf{x}_d^+(j)$.

8. If the geometric error (sum-of-squares of weighted innovations $\boldsymbol{\nu}_i(j)^\top R_i(j)^{-1} \boldsymbol{\nu}_i(j)$) is reduced, reduce λ (say by a factor of 10). Otherwise the iteration failed to reduce the error, so increase λ (e.g. multiply by 10) and reset the reconstruction to the old values $P(j)$, $\mathbf{X}_i$.

9. If a termination criterion has been met (e.g. on the reduction of the error), exit, else return to step 1.

8 Results

Details of the projective bundle adjustment algorithms implemented in other work is sketchy. We have designed two alternative approaches with features similar to [6] and [3], and which fit into the classification scheme of Triggs [19] as follows:

Elimination: in this method we enforce a canonical frame $P(j)$ set to $(I_{3\times3}|\mathbf{0})$, and fix other elements of the projection matrices and structure vectors so as to reduce the parameters to a minimal representation. The canonical frame is enforced in [6].

Free Gauge: here we employ the full represenation without any constraints. The matrix pseudo-inverse is employed in the update (6), a method that is known to give optimal results for Euclidean reconstruction ([9] page 97). The free gauge method is employed in [3].

Figure 1 compares the progress of Levenberg-Marquardt iterations in minimising the total sum-of-squares of image projection errors, for a simulated data set of 10 images of 20 3D points set within a sphere, with 5% of projected features randomly chosen to be "invisible". Gaussian noise with standard deviation 0.5 pixel is added to each image coordinate. The starting point is the same in all cases, and is provided using the fundamental matrix method described in [11]. Two runs of our normalisation method are shown, with different initial projective coordinate frames. These graphs coincide, demonstrating the invariance of the algorithm to coordinate frame. To show the effect of the arbitrary choices in the elimination and free gauge methods, we also obtained results for two runs of each, in which the order of the images was reversed in the case of elimination, and a different coordinate frame used for the second run of the free gauge method. The results demonstrate the drastic effect this can have, even with excellent input data like this. The oscillations in all four of the runs of the alternative approaches are a typical problem with the Levenberg-Marquardt algorithm in badly conditioned systems, and are

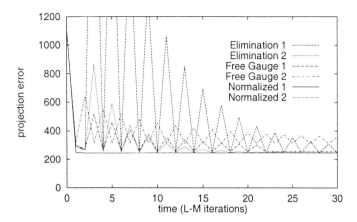

Figure 1. Results for simulated data set. The "Normalized" graphs show two (indistinguishable) results for our algorithm starting in different coordinate frames. Two runs of alternative "Elimination" and "Free Gauge" methods are also shown for comparison.

linked to oscillations in the value of λ as it tries to find the right balance between inverse Hessian and gradient descent minimization schemes. Our "Normalized" algorithm converges to the solution in five iterations, whereas the convergence of the other methods is variable and unpredictable. In terms of efficiency, the "Elimination" method was fastest, at 9.7 sec for the complete run of 30 iterations on a PC with a 233MHz AMD K6. Our favoured "Normalized" algorithm took 18.6 sec, and the "Free Gauge" approach took 83.1 sec because of the expensive SVD used to compute the pseudo-inverse.

9 Conclusions

We have demonstrated that a simple normalization applied to projective camera matrices (or structure vectors) can markedly improve projective bundle adjustment. Software to implement invariant projective bundle adjustment incorporated with the VSDF algorithm [11] is available from the Horatio WWW home page at

http://www.ee.surrey.ac.uk/Personal/

P.McLauchlan/horatio/html/index.html

In future work we shall show how to extend the ideas to Euclidean and affine reconstruction, and also to other features such as lines and planes.

References

[1] A. Azarbayejani and A. P. Pentland. Recursive estimation of motion, structure, and focal length. *IEEE Transactions on Pattern Analysis and Machine Intelligence*, 17(6):562–575, 1995.

[2] R. Berthilsson, A. Heyden, and G. Sparr. Recursive structure and motion from image sequences using shape and depth spaces. In *Proc. of the IEEE Conf. on Computer Vision and Pattern Recognition*, 1997.

[3] A. Fitzgibbon and A. Zisserman. Automatic camera recovery for closed or open image sequences. In *Proc. 5th European Conf. on Computer Vision, Freiburg*, volume 1, pages 311–326. Springer-Verlag, June 1998.

[4] G. H. Golub and C. F. van Loan. *Matrix Computations, 3rd edition*. The John Hopkins University Press, Baltimore, MD, 1996.

[5] R. Hartley. Euclidean reconstruction from uncalibrated views. In *Applications of Invariance in Computer Vision*, pages 237–256. Springer-Verlag, 1994.

[6] R. I. Hartley. Projective reconstruction and invariants from multiple images. *IEEE Transactions on Pattern Analysis and Machine Intelligence*, 16(10):1036–1041, Oct. 1994.

[7] R. I. Hartley. In defence of the 8-point algorithm. In *Proc. 5th Int'l Conf. on Computer Vision, Boston*, pages 1064–1070, 1995.

[8] A. Heyden. Projective reconstruction from image sequqnces using factorization methods - a generic approash. Submitted to PAMI, 1998.

[9] H. M. Karara. *Non-Topographic Photogrammetry*. Americal Society for Photogrammetry and Remote Sensing, 1989.

[10] Q.-T. Luong and T. Viéville. Canonic representations for the geometries of multiple projective views. In *Proc. 3rd European Conf. on Computer Vision, Stockholm*, pages 589–599, May 1994.

[11] P. McLauchlan and D. Murray. A unifying framework for structure and motion recovery from image sequences. In *Proc. 5th Int'l Conf. on Computer Vision, Boston*, pages 314–320, June 1995.

[12] P. F. McLauchlan, X. Shen, P. Palmer, A. Manessis, and A. Hilton. Surface-based structure-from-motion using feature groupings. Submitted to ICCV'99, Corfu, 1999.

[13] P.A.Beardsley, A.Zisserman, and D.W.Murray. Sequential updating of projective and affine structure from motion. *International Journal of Computer Vision*, 23(3), 1997.

[14] W. Press, B. Flannery, S. Teukolsky, and W. Vetterling. *Numerical Recipes in C*. Cambridge University Press, 1988.

[15] L. Quan and T. Kanade. Affine structure from line correspondences with uncalibrated affine cameras. *IEEE Transactions on Pattern Analysis and Machine Intelligence*, 19(8):834–845, 1997.

[16] C. Slama, C. Theurer, and S. Henriksen, editors. *Manual of Photogrammetry*. American Society of Photogrammetry, 1980.

[17] P. Sturm and B. Triggs. A factorization-based algorithm for multi-image projective structure and motion. In *Proc. 4th European Conf. on Computer Vision, Cambridge*. Springer-Verlag, 1996.

[18] C. Tomasi and T. Kanade. Shape and motion from image streams under orthography: A factorization approach. *International Journal of Computer Vision*, 9(2):137–154, 1992.

[19] B. Triggs. Optimal estimation of matching constraints. In *Proc. SMILE Workshop (associated with ECCV'98)*, 1998.

Session III

Image-Based Modeling—
Photometry

Illumination-Based Image Synthesis: Creating Novel Images of Human Faces Under Differing Pose and Lighting*

Athinodoros S. Georghiades   Peter N. Belhumeur

Center for Computational Vision and Control
Yale University
New Haven, CT 06520-8267

David J. Kriegman

Beckman Institute
University of Illinois, Urbana-Champaign
Urbana, IL 61801

Abstract

We present an illumination-based method for synthesizing images of an object under novel viewing conditions. Our method requires as few as three images of the object taken under variable illumination, but from a fixed viewpoint. Unlike multi-view based image synthesis, our method does not require the determination of point or line correspondences. Furthermore, our method is able to synthesize not simply novel viewpoints, but novel illumination conditions as well. We demonstrate the effectiveness of our approach by generating synthetic images of human faces.

1 Introduction

We present an illumination-based method for creating novel images of an object under differing pose and lighting. This method uses as few as three images of the object taken under variable lighting but fixed pose to estimate the object's albedo and generate its geometric structure. Our approach does not require any knowledge about the light source directions in the modeling images, or the establishment of point or line correspondences.

In contrast, nearly all approaches to view synthesis or image-based rendering take a set of images gathered from multiple viewpoints and apply techniques akin to structure from motion [17, 28, 6], stereopsis [21, 9], image transfer [3], image warping [18, 20, 24], or image morphing [7, 23]. Each of these methods requires the establishment of correspondence between image data (e.g. pixels) across the set. (Unlike other methods, the Lumigraph [12, 19] exhaustively samples the ray space and renders images of an object from novel viewpoints by taking $2-D$ slices of the $4-D$ light field at the appropriate directions.) Since dense correspondence is difficult to obtain, most methods extract sparse image features (e.g. corners, lines), and may use multi-view geometric constraints (e.g. the trifocal tensor [2, 1]) or scene-dependent geometric constraints

[9, 8] to reduce the search process and constrain the estimates. By using a sequence of images taken at nearby viewpoints, incremental tracking can further simplify the process, particularly when features are sparse.

For these approaches to be effective, there must be sufficient texture or viewpoint-independent scene features, such as albedo discontinuities or surface normal discontinuities. From sparse correspondence, the epipolar geometry can be established and stereo techniques can be used to provide dense reconstruction. Underlying nearly all such stereo algorithms is a constant brightness assumption – that is, the intensity (irradiance) of corresponding pixels should be the same. In turn, constant brightness implies two seldom stated assumptions: (1) The scene is Lambertian, and (2) the lighting is static with respect to the scene – only the viewpoint is changing.

In the presented illumination-based approach, we also assume that the surface is Lambertian, although this assumption is very explicit. As a dual to the second point listed above, our method requires that the camera remains static with respect to the scene – only the lighting is changing. As a consequence, geometric correspondence is trivially established, and so the method can be applied to scenes where it is difficult to establish multi-viewpoint correspondence, namely scenes that are highly textured (i.e. where image features are not sparse) or scenes that completely lack texture (i.e. where there are insufficient image features).

At the core of our approach for generating novel viewpoints is a variant of photometric stereo [27, 29, 14, 13, 30] which simultaneously estimates geometry and albedo across the scene. However, the main limitation of classical photometric stereo is that the light source positions must be accurately known, and this necessitates a fixed lighting rig as might be possible in an industrial setting. Instead, the proposed method *does not* require knowledge of light source locations, and so illumination could be varied by simply waiving a light around the scene.

In fact, our method derives from work by Belhumeur and Kriegman in [5] where they showed that a small set of images with unknown light source directions can

---

*P. N. Belhumeur and A. S. Georghiades were supported by a Presidential Early Career Award, an NSF Career Award IRI-9703134, and ARO grant DAAH04-95-1-0494. D. J. Kriegman was supported by NSF under NYI, IRI-9257990, and by ARO grant DAAG55-98-1-0168.

47

be used to generate a representation – the illumination cone – which models the complete set of images of an object (in fixed pose) under all possible illumination. This method had as its pre-cursor the work of Shashua [25] who showed that, in the absence of shadows, the set of images of an object lies in a $3 - D$ subspace in the image space. Generated images from the illumination cone representation accurately depict shading and attached shadows under extreme lighting; in [11] the cone representation was extended to include cast shadows (shadows the object casts on itself) for objects with non-convex shapes. Unlike attached shadows, cast shadows are global effects, and their prediction requires the reconstruction of the object's surface.

In generating the geometric structure, multi-viewpoint methods typically estimate depth directly from corresponding image points [21, 9]. It is well known that without sub-pixel correspondence, stereopsis provides a modest number of disparities over the effective operating range, and so smoothness or regularization constraints are used to interpolate and provide smooth surfaces. The presented illumination-based method estimates surface normals which are then integrated to generate a surface. As a result, very subtle changes in depth are recovered as demonstrated in the synthetic images in Figures 4 and 5. Those images show also the effectiveness of our approach in generating realistic images of faces under novel pose and illumination conditions.

2 Illumination Modeling

In [5], Belhumeur and Kriegman have shown that, for a convex object with a Lambertian reflectance function, the set of all images under an arbitrary combination of point light sources forms a convex polyhedral cone in the image space $\mathbb{R}^n$ which can be constructed with as few as three images.

Let $\mathbf{x} \in \mathbb{R}^n$ denote an image with n pixels of a convex object with a Lambertian reflectance function illuminated by a single point source at infinity. Let $B \in \mathbb{R}^{n \times 3}$ be a matrix where each row in B is the product of the albedo with the inward pointing unit normal for a point on the surface projecting to a particular pixel in the image. A point light source at infinity can be represented by $\mathbf{s} \in \mathbb{R}^3$ signifying the product of the light source intensity with a unit vector in the direction of the light source. A convex Lambertian surface with normals and albedo given by B, illuminated by $\mathbf{s}$, produces an image $\mathbf{x}$ given by

$$\mathbf{x} = \max(B\mathbf{s}, \mathbf{0}), \qquad (1)$$

where $\max(B\mathbf{s}, \mathbf{0})$ sets to zero all negative components of the vector $B\mathbf{s}$. The pixels set to zero correspond to the surface points lying in an attached shadow. Convexity of the object's shape is assumed at this point to avoid cast shadows. It should be noted that when no part of the surface is shadowed, $\mathbf{x}$ lies in the 3-D subspace $\mathcal{L}$ given by the span of the columns of B.

If an object is illuminated by k light sources at infinity, then the image is given by the superposition of the images which would have been produced by the individual light sources, i.e.,

$$\mathbf{x} = \sum_{i=1}^{k} \max(B\mathbf{s}_i, \mathbf{0}) \qquad (2)$$

where $\mathbf{s}_i$ is a single light source. Due to the inherent superposition, it follows that the set of all possible images $\mathcal{C}$ of a convex Lambertian surface created by varying the direction and strength of an arbitrary number of point light sources at infinity is a convex cone. It is also evident from Equation 2 that this convex cone is completely described by matrix B.

This suggests a way to construct the illumination model for an individual: gather three or more images of the face without shadowing illuminated by a single light source at unknown locations but viewed under fixed pose, and use them to estimate the three-dimensional illumination subspace $\mathcal{L}$. This can be done by first normalizing the images to unit length and then estimating the best three-dimensional orthogonal basis B^* using a least-squares minimization technique such as singular value decomposition (SVD). Note that the basis B^* differs from B by an unknown linear transformation, i.e., $B = B^* A$ where $A \in GL(3)$ [10, 13, 22]; for any light source $\mathbf{s}$, $\mathbf{x} = B\mathbf{s} = (B^* A)(A^{-1}\mathbf{s})$. Nevertheless, both B^* and B define the same illumination cone and represent valid illumination models.

Unfortunately, using SVD in the above procedure leads to an inaccurate estimate of B^*. For even a convex object whose Gaussian image covers the Gauss sphere, there is only one light source direction (the viewing direction) for which no point on the surface is in shadow. For any other light source direction, shadows will be present. If the object is non-convex, such as a face, then shadowing in the modeling images is likely to be more pronounced. When SVD is used to find B^* from images with shadows, these systematic errors bias its estimate significantly. Therefore, an alternative way is needed to find B^* that takes into account the fact that some data values should not be used in the estimation.

We have implemented a variation of [26] (see also [28, 16]) that finds a basis B^* for the 3-D linear subspace $\mathcal{L}$ from image data with missing elements. To begin, define the data matrix for c images of an individual to be $X = [\mathbf{x}_1 \ldots \mathbf{x}_c]$. If there were no shadowing, X would be rank 3 (assuming no image noise), and we could use SVD to factorize X into $X = B^* S^*$ where S^* is a $3 \times c$ matrix the columns of which are the light source directions scaled by the light intensities $\mathbf{s}_i$ for all c images.

Since the images have shadows (both cast and attached), and possibly saturations, we first have to determine which data values are invalid. Unlike saturations which can be trivially determined, finding shadows is more involved. In our implementation, a pixel is assigned to be in shadow if its value divided by its corresponding albedo is below a threshold. As an initial estimate of the albedo, we use the average of the modeling (or training) images. A conservative threshold is then chosen to determine shadows making it almost certain no invalid data is included in the estimation process, at the small expense of throwing away some valid data. After finding the invalid data, the following estimation method is used: without doing any row or column permutations sift out all the full rows (with no invalid data) of matrix X to form a full sub-matrix $\tilde{X}$. Note that the number of pixels in an image (i.e. the number of rows of X) is much larger than the number of images (i.e. the number of columns of X), which means we can always find a large number of full rows so that the number of rows of $\tilde{X}$ is larger than its number of columns. Therefore, perform SVD on $\tilde{X}$ to get a fairly good initial estimate of S^*. Fix S^* and estimate each of the rows of B^* independently using least squares. Then, fix B^* and update each of the light source direction $\mathbf{s}_i$ independently, again using least squares. Repeat these last two steps until estimates converge. In our experiments, the algorithm is very well behaved, converging to the global minimum within 10-15 iterations. Though it is possible to converge to a local minimum, we never observed this either in simulation or in practice.

Figure 1 demonstrates the process for constructing the illumination model. Figure 1.a shows six of the original single light source images of a face used in the estimation of B^*. Note that the light source in each image moves only by a small amount ($\pm 15^o$ in either direction) about the viewing axis. Despite this, the images do exhibit shadowing, e.g. left and right of the nose. In fact, there is a tradeoff in the image acquisition process: the smaller the motion of the light source, meaning fewer shadows present in the images, the worse the conditioning of the estimation problem. If, on the other hand, the light source moves excessively, despite the improvement in the conditioning, more extensive shadowing can increase the possibility of having too few (less than three) valid measurements with a fixed number of images for some parts of the face. Therefore, the light source should move in moderation as in the images shown in Figure 1.a.

Figure 1.b shows the basis images of the estimated matrix B^*. These basis images encode not only the albedo (reflectance) of the face but also its surface normal field. They can be used to construct images of the face under arbitrary and quite extreme illumination conditions. However, the image formation model in Equation 1 does not account for cast shadows of non-convex objects such as faces. In order to determine which parts of the image are in cast shadows, given a light source direction, we need to reconstruct the surface of the face (see next section) and then use ray-tracing techniques.

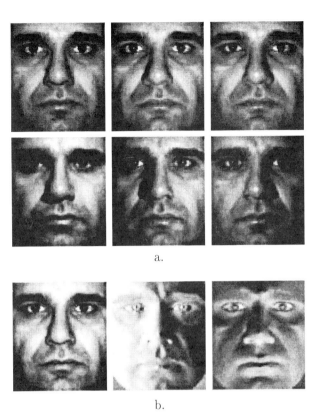

a.

b.

Figure 1: a) Six of the original single light source images used to estimate B^*. Note that the light source in each image moves only by a small amount ($\pm 15^o$ in either direction) about the viewing axis. Despite this, the images do exhibit shadowing. b) The basis images of B^*.

3 Surface Reconstruction

In this section, we demonstrate how we can generate an object's surface from B^* after enforcing the integrability constraint on the surface normal field. It has been shown [4, 31] that from multiple images, in which the light source directions are unknown, one can only recover a Lambertian surface up to a three-parameter family given by the generalized bas-relief (GBR) transformation. This family scales the relief (flattens or extrudes) and introduces an additive plane. It has also been shown that the family of GBR transformations is the only one that preserves integrability.

3.1 Enforcing Integrability

The vector field B^* estimated in Section 2 may not be integrable, i.e., it may not correspond to a smooth surface. So, prior to reconstructing the surface up to GBR, the integrability constraint must be enforced on B^*. Since no method has been developed to enforce the integrability during the estimation of B^*, we enforce it afterwards. That is, given B^* estimate a matrix $A \in GL(3)$ such that $\hat{B} = B^*A$ corresponds to an integrable normal field; the development follows [31].

Consider a continuous surface defined as the graph of $z(x, y)$, and let $\mathbf{b}(x, y)$ be the corresponding normal field scaled by an albedo field. The integrability constraint for a surface is $z_{xy} = z_{yx}$ where subscripts denote partial derivatives. In turn, $\mathbf{b}(x,y)$ must satisfy:

$$\left(\frac{b_1}{b_3}\right)_y = \left(\frac{b_2}{b_3}\right)_x$$

To estimate A such that $\mathbf{b}^T(x,y) = \mathbf{b}^{*T}(x,y)A$, we expand this out. Letting the columns of A be denoted by A_1, A_2, A_3 yields

$$(\mathbf{b}^{*T}A_3)(\mathbf{b}_x^{*T}A_2) - (\mathbf{b}^{*T}A_2)(\mathbf{b}_x^{*T}A_3) =$$
$$(\mathbf{b}^{*T}A_3)(\mathbf{b}_y^{*T}A_1) - (\mathbf{b}^{*T}A_1)(\mathbf{b}_y^{*T}A_3)$$

which can be expressed as

$$\mathbf{b}^{*T}S_1\mathbf{b}_x^* = \mathbf{b}^{*T}S_2\mathbf{b}_y^* \qquad (3)$$

where $S_1 = A_3A_2^T - A_2A_3^T$ and $S_2 = A_3A_1^T - A_1A_3^T$.

S_1 and S_2 are skew-symmetric matrices and have three degrees of freedom. Equation 3 is linear in the six elements of S_1 and S_2. From the estimate of B^* discrete approximations of the partial derivatives ($\mathbf{b}_x^*$ and $\mathbf{b}_y^*$) are computed, and then SVD is used to solve for the six elements of S_1 and S_2. In [31], it was shown that the elements of S_1 and S_2 are cofactors of A, and a simple method for computing A from the cofactors was presented. This procedure only determines six degrees of freedom of A. The other three correspond to the GBR transformation [4] and can be chosen arbitrarily because a GBR transformation preserves integrability. The surface corresponding to $\hat{B} = B^*A$ differs from the true surface by GBR, i.e., $\hat{z}(x,y) = \lambda z(x,y) + \mu x + \nu y$ for arbitrary λ, μ, ν with $\lambda \neq 0$.

3.2   Generating a GBR surface

After enforcing integrability, we can now reconstruct the corresponding surface $\hat{z}(x,y)$. Note that $\hat{z}(x,y)$ is not a Euclidean reconstruction of the face, but a representative element of the orbit under a GBR transformation. Despite this, both the shading *and* the shadowing will be correct for images synthesized from such a surface [4].

To find $\hat{z}(x,y)$, we use the variational approach presented in [15]. A surface $\hat{z}(x,y)$ is fit to the given components of the gradient p and q by minimizing the functional

$$\int\int_{\Omega} (\hat{z}_x - p)^2 + (\hat{z}_y - q)^2 \, dx \, dy.$$

the Euler equation of which reduces to $\nabla^2 z = p_x + q_y$. By enforcing the right natural boundary conditions and employing an iterative scheme that uses a discrete approximation of the Laplacian, we can reconstruct the surface $\hat{z}(x,y)$ [15].

Recall that a GBR transformation scales the relief (flattens or extrudes) and introduces an additive plane. To resolve this GBR ambiguity, we take advantage of the fact that we are dealing with human faces which constitute a well known class of objects. We can therefore exploit the left-to-right symmetry of faces and the fairly constant ratios of distances between facial features such as the eyes, the nose, and the forehead. (In the case when the class of objects is not well defined, the issue of resolving the GBR ambiguity becomes more subtle and is essentially an open problem.) A surface of a face that has undergone a GBR transformation will have different distance ratios and can be asymmetric. These differences allow us to estimate the three parameters of the GBR transformation which we can then invert. Note that this inverse transformation is applied to both the estimated surface $\hat{z}(x,y)$ and $\hat{B}$. Even though this inverse operation (which is also a GBR transformation) may not completely resolve the ambiguity of the relief because of errors in the estimation of the GBR parameters, it nevertheless comes very close to that effect. After all, our purpose is not to reconstruct the exact Euclidean surface of the face, but to create realistic images of a face under differing pose and illumination. Moreover, since shadows are preserved under GBR transformations [4], images synthesized under an arbitrary light source from a surface whose normal field has been GBR transformed will have correct shadowing. This means that the residual GBR transformation (after resolving the ambiguity) will not affect the image synthesis with variable illumination.

Figure 2 shows the reconstructed surface of the face shown in Figure 1 after resolving the GBR ambiguity. The first basis image of B^* shown in Figure 1.b has been texture-mapped on the surface. Even though we cannot recover the exact Euclidean structure of the face (i.e. resolve the ambiguity completely), we can still generate synthetic images of a face under variable pose where the shape distortions due to the residual GBR ambiguity are quite small and not visually detectable.

4   Image Synthesis

We first demonstrate the ability of our method to generate images of an object under novel illumination conditions but fixed pose. Figure 3 shows sample single light source images of a face generated with the image formation model in Equation 1 which has been extended to account for cast shadows. To determine cast shadows, we employ ray-tracing that uses the reconstructed surface of the face $\hat{z}(x,y)$ after resolving the GBR ambiguity. Specifically, a point on the surface is in cast shadow if, for a given light source direction, a ray emanating from that point parallel to the light source direction intersects the surface at some other point. With this extended image formation model, the generated images exhibit realistic shading and, despite the small presence of shadows in the images in Figure 1.a, have strong attached and cast shadows.

Figure 4 displays a set of synthesized images of the

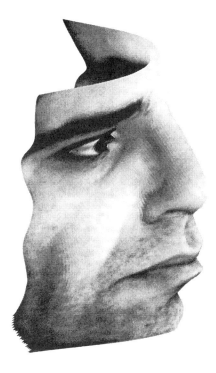

Figure 2: The reconstructed surface.

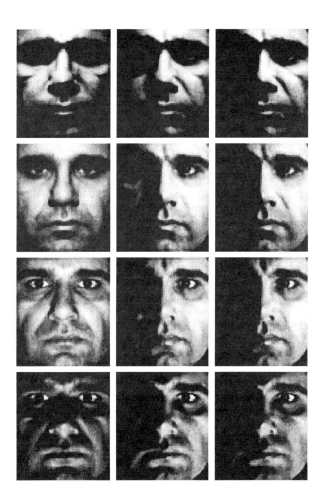

Figure 3: Sample images of the face under novel illumination conditions but fixed pose.

the face viewed under variable pose but with fixed lighting. The images were created by rigidly rotating the reconstructed surface shown in Figure 2 first about the horizontal and then about the vertical axis. Along the rows from left to right, the azimuth varies (in 10 degree intervals) from 30 degrees to the right of the face to 10 degrees to the left. Down the columns, the elevation varies (again in 10 degree intervals) from 20 degrees above the horizon to 30 degrees below. For example, in the bottom image of the second column from the left the surface has an azimuth of 20 degrees to the right and an elevation of 30 degrees below the horizon. The single light source is following the face around as it changes pose. This implies that a patch on the surface has the same intensity in all poses. It is interesting to see that the images look quite realistic with maybe the exception of the three right images in the bottom row which appear to be a little flattened. This is not due to any errors during the geometric or photometric modeling but probably due to our visual priors; we are not used to looking at a face from above.

In Figure 5, we combine both variations in viewing conditions to synthesize images of the face under novel pose and lighting. We used the same poses as in Figure 4 but now the light from the single point source is fixed to come along the gaze direction of the face in the top-right image. Therefore, as the face moves around and its gaze direction changes with respect to the light source direction, the shading of the surface changes and both attached and cast shadows are formed, as one would expect. The synthesized images seem to agree with our visual intuition.

5 Discussion

Appearance variation of an object caused by small changes in illumination under fixed pose can provide enough information to estimate (under the assumption of a Lambertian reflectance function) the object's surface normal field scaled by its albedo. In the presented method, as few as three images with no knowledge of the light source directions can be used in the estimation. The estimated surface normal field can then be integrated to reconstruct the object's surface. Unlike multi-view based image synthesis, our approach does not require the determination of point or line correspondences to do the surface reconstruction. Since we are dealing with a well known class of objects, we can acceptably resolve the GBR ambiguity of the reconstructed surface. Then, the surface together with the surface normal field scaled by the albedo are sufficient for synthesizing images of the object under novel pose and lighting.

The effectiveness of our approach stems from three reasons. First, the estimation of the illumination model B^* does not use any invalid data (such as shadows) which would otherwise lead to large biases. Second, the integrability constraint is enforced on the surface normal field which significantly improves the surface reconstruction. Last, unlike classical photometric stereo, our method requires no knowledge of light source locations. This obviates the need of error-prone calibration of a fixed lighting rig where any errors in estimating the position of the light sources can propagate to the estimation of the illumination model causing large inaccuracies. These reasons have to led to improved performance and we have demonstrated this by synthesizing realistic images of human faces.

References

[1] S. Avidan, T. Evgeniou, A. Shashua, and T. Poggio. Image-based view synthesis by combining trilinear tensors and learning techniques. In *ACM Symposium on Virtual Reality Software and Technology*, 1997.

[2] S. Avidan and A. Shashua. Novel view synthesis in tensor space. In *Proc. IEEE Conf. on Comp. Vision and Patt. Recog.*, pages 1034–1040, 1997.

[3] E. Barett, M. Brill, N. Haag, and P. Payton. Invariant linear methods in photogrammetry and model matching. In J. Mundy and A. Zisserman, editors, *Geometric Invariance in Computer Vision*, pages 277–292. MIT Press, 1992.

[4] P. Belhumeur, D. Kriegman, and A. Yuille. The bas-relief ambiguity. In *Proc. IEEE Conf. on Comp. Vision and Patt. Recog.*, pages 1040–1046, 1997.

[5] P. N. Belhumeur and D. J. Kriegman. What is the set of images of an object under all possible lighting conditions? In *Proc. IEEE Conf. on Comp. Vision and Patt. Recog.*, pages 270–277, 1996.

[6] R. Carceroni and K. Kutulakos. Shape and motion of 3-d curves from multi-view image scenes. In *Image Understanding Workshop*, pages 171–176, 1998.

[7] S. Chen and L. Williams. View interpolation for image synthesis. In *Computer Graphics (SIGGRAPH)*, pages 279–288, 1993.

[8] G. Chou and S. Teller. Multi-image correspondence using geometric and structural constraints. In *Image Understanding Workshop*, pages 869–874, 1997.

[9] P. Debevec, C. Taylor, and J. Malik. Modeling and rendering architecture from photographs: A hybrid geometry- and image-based approach. In *Computer Graphics (SIGGRAPH)*, pages 11–20, 1996.

[10] R. Epstein, A. Yuille, and P. N. Belhumeur. Learning and recognizing objects using illumination subspaces. In *Proc. of the Int. Workshop on Object Representation for Computer Vision*, 1996.

[11] A. Georghiades, D. Kriegman, and P. Belhumeur. Illumination cones for recognition under variable lighting: Faces. In *Proc. IEEE Conf. on Comp. Vision and Patt. Recog.*, 1998.

[12] S. J. Gortler, R. Grzeszczuk, R. Szeliski, and M. F. Cohen. The Lumigraph. In *Computer Graphics (SIGGRAPH)*, pages 43–54, 1996.

[13] H. Hayakawa. Photometric stereo under a light-source with arbitrary motion. *JOSA-A*, 11(11):3079–3089, Nov. 1994.

[14] B. Horn. *Computer Vision*. MIT Press, Cambridge, Mass., 1986.

[15] B. Horn and M. Brooks. The variational approach to shape from shading. *Computer Vision, Graphics and Image Processing*, 35:174–208, 1992.

[16] D. Jacobs. Linear fitting with missing data: Applications to structure from motion and characterizing intensity images. In *Proc. IEEE Conf. on Comp. Vision and Patt. Recog.*, 1997.

[17] J. Koenderink and A. Van Doorn. Affine structure from motion. *JOSA-A*, 8(2):377–385, 1991.

[18] S. Laveau and O. Faugeras. 3-D scene representation as a collection of images and fundamental matrices. Technical Report 2205, INRIA-Sophia Antipolis, February 1994.

[19] M. Levoy and P. Hanrahan. Light field rendering. In *Computer Graphics (SIGGRAPH)*, pages 31–42, 1996.

[20] W. R. Mark, L. McMillan, and G. Bishop. Post-rendering 3d warping. In *Computer Graphics (SIGGRAPH)*, pages 39–46, 1997.

[21] L. Matthies, R. Szeliski, and T. Kanade. Kalman filter-based algorithms for estimating depth from image sequences. *Int. J. Computer Vision*, 3:293–312, 1989.

[22] R. Rosenholtz and J. Koenderink. Affine structure and photometry. In *Proc. IEEE Conf. on Comp. Vision and Patt. Recog.*, pages 790–795, 1996.

[23] S. Seitz and C. Dyer. View morphing. In *Computer Graphics (SIGGRAPH)*, pages 21–30, 1996.

[24] J. Shade, S. Gortler, L. wei He, and R. Szeliski. Layered depth maps. In *Computer Graphics (SIGGRAPH)*, pages 251–258, 1998.

[25] A. Shashua. *Geometry and Photometry in 3D Visual Recognition*. PhD thesis, MIT, 1992.

[26] H. Shum, K. Ikeuchi, and R. Reddy. Principal component analysis with missing data and its application to polyhedral object modeling. *IEEE Trans. Pattern Anal. Mach. Intelligence*, 17(9):854–867, September 1995.

[27] W. Silver. *Determining Shape and Reflectance Using Multiple Images*. PhD thesis, MIT, Cambridge, MA, 1980.

[28] C. Tomasi and T. Kanade. Shape and motion from image streams under orthography: A factorization method. *Int. J. Computer Vision*, 9(2):137–154, 1992.

[29] R. Woodham. Analysing images of curved surfaces. *Artificial Intelligence*, 17:117–140, 1981.

[30] Y. Yu and J. Malik. Recovering photometric properties of architectural scenes from photographs. In *Computer Graphics (SIGGRAPH)*, pages 207–218, 1998.

[31] A. Yuille and D. Snow. Shape and albedo from multiple images using integrability. In *Proc. IEEE Conf. on Comp. Vision and Patt. Recog.*, pages 158–164, 1997.

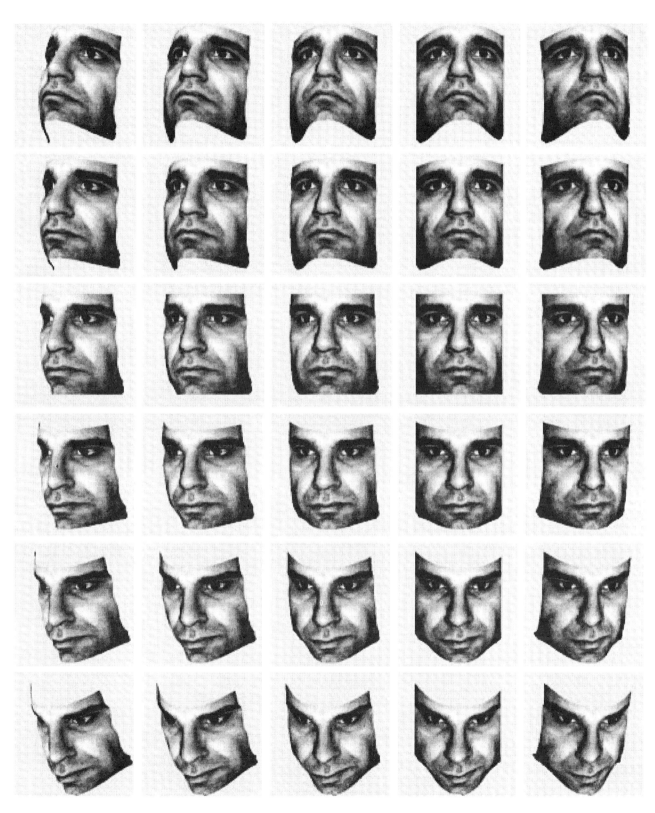

Figure 4: Synthesized images under variable pose but with fixed lighting; the single light source is following the face.

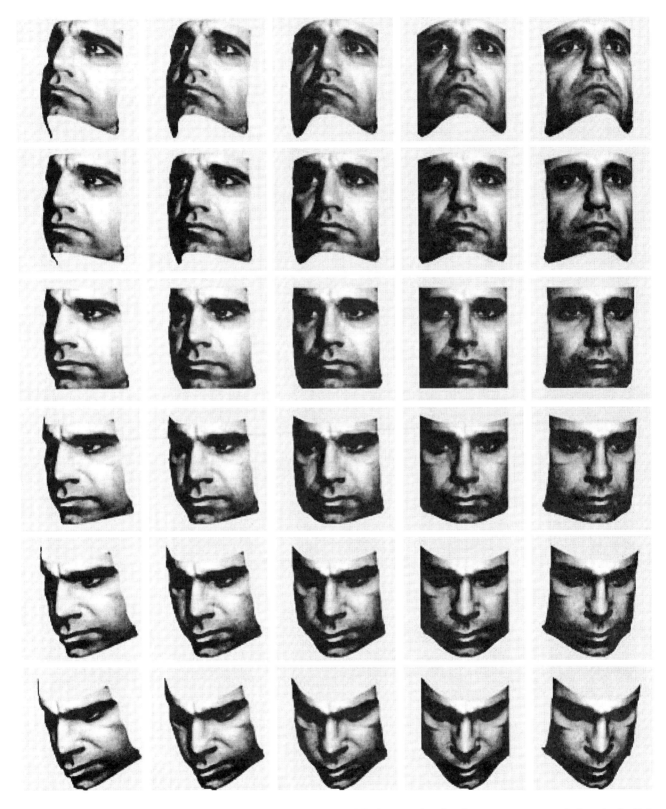

Figure 5: Synthesized images under *both* variable pose and lighting. As the face moves around the single light source stays fixed resulting to image variability due to changes in pose and illumination conditions.

The Linear Geo-Photometric Constraint for Image Matching, Structure Reconstruction, Image Synthesis and Object Recognition

Gang Xu and Guodong Guo*
Computer Vision Lab, Computer Science Department
Ritsumeikan University, Kusatsu, Shiga 525-8577, Japan
*Now with Nanyang Technological University, Singapore

Abstract

In this paper we show that under orthographic projection (can be relaxed to weak perspective, or scaled orthographic projection) and with a fixed camera and fixed light sources, the images of a moving Lambertian surface can be modelled as a linear combination of three distinct images, with identical coefficients for both shape and intensity. We call this the linear geo-photometric constraint. Using this new constraint, we can match images, reconstruct structure, synthesize new images and recognize objects. Experimental results are shown.

1 Introduction

It has been shown by Ullman and Basri that the image coordinates of a point are linear combinations of the image coordinates of the corresponding points in three other distinct images, under affine projections [14, 11]. It has also been shown by Shashua and Belhumeur et al. that the intensity of an image point is a linear combination of the intensities of the same point in three other distinct images, assuming Lambertian surfaces [11, 1]. However, it was not clear how these two linear combinations relate to each other. In this paper, we show that actually, the coefficients of both linear combination equations are identical under fixed camera and fixed light sources. It applies to color as well. We call this the *Linear Geo-Photometric Constraint* or simply LGPC.

It should be noted that for multiple views, the trifocal tensors or trilinearity are the most general concept which not only accounts for the affine projection but also for the full perspective projection [12, 6]. In this paper, however, we only deal with the weak perspective projection, because only under this assumption, do the shape and shading share the same linear combination equations.

Any linear combination theory (and the trilinearity theory as well) inherently requires the images be matched first. Most stereo matchers, and Ullman et al. who developed the linear combination theory for shape, assume that the intensities of the corresponding points do not change over images so that the correlation techniques or optical flow techniques can be applied for matching [14]. On the other hand, Shuasha and Belhumeur et al. show that the intensity does change as a linear combination of three distinct base images when the light source moves [11, 1]. When only the light source moves, that is, the camera and object do not move, there is no image matching problem involved. However, when the object moves, though the linear combination theory still holds, one needs to solve the correspondence problem. All this being said, one realizes that we need to incorporate the constraint for intensity variability into matching.

As far as we know, the first attempt along this line is the work by Maki *et al* [9]. They compute the linear combination of intensities for each matched point in three base images and search for the corresponding point in a fourth image which is required to have the predicted intensity. Their work make use of, rather than reject, the intensity change for matching. However, there is a problem regarding how to determine the coefficients of the linear combination at the first place. They claim that the coefficients can be determined from the intensities of the matched feature points. However, it is known that the intensities of feature points are extremely unreliable for such a purpose. Using LGPC, on the other hand, it is very easy to determine the coefficients, because the coeffients for intensity are the same for point positions, which can be reliably located. In both cases, we need to first match a few (≥ 4) feature points using feature point tracking [13], or the epipolar constraint [15].

With the coefficients determined, we can simultaneously match the images and reconstruct the structure. Now we are given a fourth image. If more than 4 feature points are matched over all the 4 images, we can determine the motions between them up to a scale and reflection [7, 13, 16]. For any point in, say, the first image, we can assume a depth and then the 3D point is projected onto other 3 images. For the assumed depth to be correct, the 4 corresponding points must satisfy the linear geo-photometric constraint. Again the smoothness constraint is required to play a role, as LGPC alone does not give a unique solution. The result is a simultaneous determination of correspondence and depth for each point. In this paper, we show a new algorithm based on LGPC.

Another area where LGPC can be applied is image synthesis. Given an arbitrary rotation of the object, the coefficients can be easily computed and the new image can be synthesized. In the case of color images, the red, green and blue channels can be synthesized separately in the same way as a grayscale image. Traditional approaches to image synthesis, like texture mapping [4], do not consider the intensity change due to pose change, but here the differences are taken into account such that the synthesized images are more photorealistic [19].

Ullman and Basri proposed the linear combination theory originally for object recognition. With the intensity for each pixel being synthesized for another pose, we can compare not only the edge maps but the whole image with the model database to see which object model has the minimal difference with input image. Here again we need to match a few feature points between the input image and models.

One final note is that a fixed camera and fixed light sources are a quite general situation.

In the following, we will first derive the LGPC equations, and then show how to use it for image correspondence, structure reconstruction, image synthesis and object recognition. Finally, preliminary experimental results are shown.

2 The Linear Geo-Photometric Constraint

We assume that both the camera and the light sources are fixed, while the object undergoes unknown motions. We also assume the orthographic projection, which is later relaxed to the weak perspective or scaled orthographic projection.

Suppose that there are n Lambertian surface points, which have 3D coordinates $\mathbf{X}_i, i = 1, ..., n$ and surface normal $\mathbf{n}_i, i = 1, ..., n$, both in a world coordinate sys-

tem. Also suppose that there are m light sources, which are far away from the object such that the directions of the light rays do not change with each surface point.

Assume that the object undergoes rotations $\mathbf{R}(j)$ and translations $\mathbf{t}(j)$, where j indicates time. Under the orthographic projection, translation along the depth direction of the camera is zero such that the object scale does not change over images.

Now we can write the coordinates and intensity of the i-th surface point in the j-th image as

$$x_i^j = \mathbf{p}_x^T(\mathbf{R}(j)\mathbf{X}_i + \mathbf{t}(j)) \quad (1)$$

$$y_i^j = \mathbf{p}_y^T(\mathbf{R}(j)\mathbf{X}_i + \mathbf{t}(j)) \quad (2)$$

$$I_i^j = \rho_i \sum_{k=1}^m \mathbf{l}_k^T \mathbf{R}(j)\mathbf{n}_i \quad (3)$$

where $\mathbf{p}_x, \mathbf{p}_y$ respectively represent the orientation of image's horizontal and vertical axes in the world coordinate system, ρ is the coefficient for the intensity scale determined by the light sources and the albedo of each point, and $\mathbf{l}_k$ represents the orientation of the k-th light source in the world coordinate system. $\mathbf{p}_x, \mathbf{p}_y$ and $\mathbf{l}_k$ are all unit vectors.

Now suppose that we have already taken 3 distinct images. For each point, we have

$$x_i^1 = \mathbf{p}_x^T(\mathbf{R}(1)\mathbf{X}_i + \mathbf{t}(1))$$

$$x_i^2 = \mathbf{p}_x^T(\mathbf{R}(2)\mathbf{X}_i + \mathbf{t}(2))$$

$$x_i^3 = \mathbf{p}_x^T(\mathbf{R}(3)\mathbf{X}_i + \mathbf{t}(3))$$

$$y_i^1 = \mathbf{p}_y^T(\mathbf{R}(1)\mathbf{X}_i + \mathbf{t}(1))$$

$$y_i^2 = \mathbf{p}_y^T(\mathbf{R}(2)\mathbf{X}_i + \mathbf{t}(2))$$

$$y_i^3 = \mathbf{p}_y^T(\mathbf{R}(3)\mathbf{X}_i + \mathbf{t}(3))$$

$$I_i^1 = \rho_i \sum_{k=1}^m \mathbf{l}_k^T \mathbf{R}(1)\mathbf{n}_i$$

$$I_i^2 = \rho_i \sum_{k=1}^m \mathbf{l}_k^T \mathbf{R}(2)\mathbf{n}_i$$

$$I_i^3 = \rho_i \sum_{k=1}^m \mathbf{l}_k^T \mathbf{R}(3)\mathbf{n}_i$$

Let us define: $\mathbf{p}_x(1) = \mathbf{R}^T(1)\mathbf{p}_x$, $\mathbf{p}_x(2) = \mathbf{R}^T(2)\mathbf{p}_x$, $\mathbf{p}_x(3) = \mathbf{R}^T(3)\mathbf{p}_x$, $\mathbf{p}_y(1) = \mathbf{R}^T(1)\mathbf{p}_y$, $\mathbf{p}_y(2) = \mathbf{R}^T(2)\mathbf{p}_y$, $\mathbf{p}_y(3) = \mathbf{R}^T(3)\mathbf{p}_y$, $\mathbf{l}_k(1) = \mathbf{R}^T(1)\mathbf{l}_k$, $\mathbf{l}_k(2) = \mathbf{R}^T(1)\mathbf{l}_k$, $\mathbf{l}_k(3) = \mathbf{R}^T(1)\mathbf{l}_k$. Provided that $\mathbf{p}_x(1), \mathbf{p}_x(2), \mathbf{p}_x(3)$ are not coplanar, the three vectors span the 3D space (Fig.1). Thus, for an arbitrary rotation $\mathbf{R}(j)$, the new vector $\mathbf{p}_x(j) = \mathbf{R}^T(j)\mathbf{p}_x$ can be represented by a linear combination of $\mathbf{p}_x(1), \mathbf{p}_x(2), \mathbf{p}_x(3)$, i.e.,

$$\mathbf{p}_x(j) = a_1(j)\mathbf{p}_x(1) + a_2(j)\mathbf{p}_x(2) + a_3(j)\mathbf{p}_x(3) \quad (4)$$

or,

$$\mathbf{p}_x(j) = \begin{bmatrix} \mathbf{p}_x(1) & \mathbf{p}_x(2) & \mathbf{p}_x(3) \end{bmatrix} \begin{bmatrix} a_1(j) \\ a_2(j) \\ a_3(j) \end{bmatrix} \quad (5)$$

where $a_1(j), a_2(j), a_3(j)$ are scalar coefficients for the j-th time. Since $\mathbf{p}_x(1)$, $\mathbf{p}_x(2)$ and $\mathbf{p}_x(3)$ are not coplanar, the coefficients can be determined by

$$\begin{bmatrix} a_1(j) \\ a_2(j) \\ a_3(j) \end{bmatrix} = \begin{bmatrix} \mathbf{p}_x(1) & \mathbf{p}_x(2) & \mathbf{p}_x(3) \end{bmatrix}^{-1} \mathbf{p}_x(j) \quad (6)$$

Geometrically, we can construct a parallel hexahedron using $\mathbf{p}_x(1)$, $\mathbf{p}_x(2)$, $\mathbf{p}_x(3)$ and $\mathbf{p}$ as in Fig.1, and $a_1(j), a_2(j)$ and $a_3(j)$ are the lengths along the directions of $\mathbf{p}_x(1)$, $\mathbf{p}_x(2)$ and $\mathbf{p}_x(3)$ of the parallel hexahedron. The lengths depend solely on the shape of the hexahedron determined by the relative orientations of the 4 vectors, while irrelevant with respect to the pose of the hexahedron.

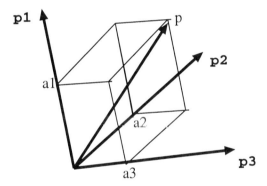

Figure 1. Three non-coplanar vectors span a 3D space. We can construct a parallel hexahedron using the 4 vectors, and $a_1(j), a_2(j)$ and $a_3(j)$ are the lengths along the directions of $\mathbf{p}_x(1)$, $\mathbf{p}_x(2)$ and $\mathbf{p}_x(3)$ of the parallel hexahedron.

Now we show that the coefficients are the same also for $\mathbf{p}_y$ and $\mathbf{l}_k$. In the world coordinate system, $\mathbf{p}_x, \mathbf{p}_y, \mathbf{l}_k$ are rigid. Furthermore, rotations $\mathbf{R}(1), \mathbf{R}(2), \mathbf{R}(3)$ do not change the spatial relations among these vectors. Thus there exist rotation matrices $\mathbf{R}_y, \mathbf{R}_k, k = 1, ..., m$ such that

$$\mathbf{p}_y = \mathbf{R}_y \mathbf{p}_x \quad (7)$$
$$\mathbf{p}_y(j) = \mathbf{R}_y \mathbf{p}_x(j) \quad (8)$$
$$\mathbf{p}_k = \mathbf{R}_k \mathbf{p}_x, \ k = 1, ..., m \quad (9)$$
$$\mathbf{p}_k(j) = \mathbf{R}_k \mathbf{p}_x(j), \ k = 1, .., m \quad (10)$$

Multiplying $\mathbf{R}_y$ and $\mathbf{R}_k, k = 1, ..., m$ from the left to both sides of (4), we have

$$\mathbf{p}_y(j) = a_1(j)\mathbf{p}_y(1) + a_2(j)\mathbf{p}_y(2) + a_3(j)\mathbf{p}_y(3) \ (11)$$
$$\mathbf{l}_k(j) = a_1(j)\mathbf{l}_k(1) + a_2(j)\mathbf{l}_k(2) + a_3(j)\mathbf{l}_k(3) \ (12)$$

It is not hard to understand as both the vectors $\mathbf{p}_y(1)$, $\mathbf{p}_y(2)$, $\mathbf{p}_y(3)$ and $\mathbf{p}_y(j)$ and the vectors $\mathbf{l}_k(1)$, $\mathbf{l}_k(2)$, $\mathbf{l}_k(3)$ and $\mathbf{l}_k(j)$ (for each k) have the same relative orientations resulting from the same rotations $\mathbf{R}(1)$, $\mathbf{R}(2)$, $\mathbf{R}(3)$ and $\mathbf{R}(j)$, and thus have the same hexahedron shape.

From (4), (11) and (12), it is straightforward to obtain

$$x_i^j = a_1(j)x_i^1 + a_2(j)x_i^2 + a_3(j)x_i^3 + a_x(j) \ (13)$$
$$y_i^j = a_1(j)y_i^1 + a_2(j)y_i^2 + a_3(j)y_i^3 + a_y(j) \ (14)$$
$$I_i^j = a_1(j)I_i^1 + a_2(j)I_i^2 + a_3(j)I_i^3 \quad (15)$$

where $a_x(j), a_y(j)$ account for translations in the horizontal and vertical image directions, respectively. If we select the centroid of the points as the image origin for each image, then $a_x = a_y = 0$.

The important thing here is that the coefficients are identical not only for the horizontal coordinate and vertical coordinate (which was not mentioned by Ullman and Basri [14]), but also for the intensity.

In the case of weak perspective projection, the object is allowed to move along the depth direction. The effect is a change of object scale in the image. As the scale change can be computed from images, we can first rescale the images such that they look like being taken under orthographic projection [10, 18, 15], and then the above equations can be applied without any modifications.

If we consider color as three independent intensity channels, the above equations apply to color as well. In that case, the equations become

$$x_i^j = a_1(j)x_i^1 + a_2(j)x_i^2 + a_3(j)x_i^3 + a_x(j) \ (16)$$
$$y_i^j = a_1(j)y_i^1 + a_2(j)y_i^2 + a_3(j)y_i^3 + a_y(j) \ (17)$$
$$R_i^j = a_1(j)R_i^1 + a_2(j)R_i^2 + a_3(j)R_i^3 \quad (18)$$
$$G_i^j = a_1(j)G_i^1 + a_2(j)G_i^2 + a_3(j)G_i^3 \quad (19)$$
$$B_i^j = a_1(j)B_i^1 + a_2(j)B_i^2 + a_3(j)B_i^3 \quad (20)$$

where R,G,B are intensities for the red, green and blue channels, respectively.

3 A new algorithm for image matching and 3D Reconstruction

3.1 Computing the coefficients

Suppose that we have taken 4 images of a moving Lambertian surface under fixed light sources with a fixed camera which is far enough from the surface such that the orthographic projection is a good approximation. We assume that a few (more than 4) feature points have been extracted and matched over the 4 images.

From (13) and (14), we have

$$\sum_{i=1}^{n} x_i^4 = a_1 \sum_{i=1}^{n} x_i^1 + a_2 \sum_{i=1}^{n} x_i^2 + a_3 \sum_{i=1}^{n} x_i^3 + \sum_{i=1}^{n} a_x$$

$$\sum_{i=1}^{n} y_i^4 = a_1 \sum_{i=1}^{n} y_i^1 + a_2 \sum_{i=1}^{n} y_i^2 + a_3 \sum_{i=1}^{n} y_i^3 + \sum_{i=1}^{n} a_y$$

This means

$$a_x = x_c^4 - (a_1 x_c^1 + a_2 x_c^2 + a_3 x_c^3) \qquad (21)$$
$$a_y = y_c^4 - (a_1 y_c^1 + a_2 y_c^2 + a_3 y_c^3) \qquad (22)$$

where $(x_c^j, y_c^j), j = 1, 2, 3, 4$, are the centroids of the corresponding feature points in the 4 images.

Substituting (21) and (22) for (13) and (14), we have

$$\tilde{x}_i^4 = a_1 \tilde{x}_i^1 + a_2 \tilde{x}_i^2 + a_3 \tilde{x}_i^3 \qquad (23)$$
$$\tilde{y}_i^4 = a_1 \tilde{y}_i^1 + a_2 \tilde{y}_i^2 + a_3 \tilde{y}_i^3 \qquad (24)$$

where

$$\tilde{x}_i^j = x_i^j - x_c^j \qquad (25)$$
$$\tilde{y}_i^j = y_i^j - y_c^j \qquad (26)$$

Now we can reformulate the original equations (13), (14) and (15) as the following:

$$\tilde{a}_1 \tilde{x}_i^1 + \tilde{a}_2 \tilde{x}_i^2 + \tilde{a}_3 \tilde{x}_i^3 + \tilde{a}_4 \tilde{x}_i^4 = 0 \qquad (27)$$
$$\tilde{a}_1 \tilde{y}_i^1 + \tilde{a}_2 \tilde{y}_i^2 + \tilde{a}_3 \tilde{y}_i^3 + \tilde{a}_4 \tilde{y}_i^4 = 0 \qquad (28)$$
$$\tilde{a}_1 \tilde{I}_i^1 + \tilde{a}_2 \tilde{I}_i^2 + \tilde{a}_3 \tilde{I}_i^3 + \tilde{a}_4 \tilde{I}_i^4 = 0 \qquad (29)$$

Given the coordinates of feature points, we obtain

$$\mathbf{X a} = \mathbf{0} \qquad (30)$$

where

$$\mathbf{X} = \begin{bmatrix} \tilde{x}_1^1 & \tilde{x}_1^2 & \tilde{x}_1^3 & \tilde{x}_1^4 \\ \tilde{y}_1^1 & \tilde{y}_1^2 & \tilde{y}_1^3 & \tilde{y}_1^4 \\ \tilde{x}_2^1 & \tilde{x}_2^2 & \tilde{x}_2^3 & \tilde{x}_2^4 \\ \tilde{y}_2^1 & \tilde{y}_2^2 & \tilde{y}_2^3 & \tilde{y}_2^4 \\ \vdots & \vdots & \vdots & \vdots \\ \tilde{x}_n^1 & \tilde{x}_n^2 & \tilde{x}_n^3 & \tilde{x}_n^4 \\ \tilde{y}_n^1 & \tilde{y}_n^2 & \tilde{y}_n^3 & \tilde{y}_n^4 \end{bmatrix}$$

and

$$\mathbf{a} = [\tilde{a}_1, \tilde{a}_2, \tilde{a}_3, \tilde{a}_4]^T$$

It is well known that $\mathbf{a}$ can be optimally determined as the eigen vector associated with the smallest eigen value of $\mathbf{X}^T \mathbf{X}$.

3.2 Simultaneous image matching and depth recovery

Given the matched feature points, we use an algorithm developed by Xu et al. to compute the 3D rotations between the images [17]. As shown in Fig.2,

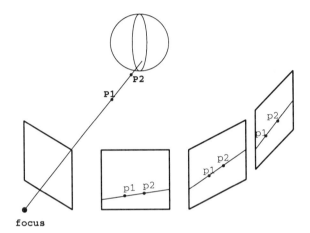

Figure 2. Changing the depth of a point in the first image moves its projection onto the other images along the epipolar lines.

since the motions are known, given any 3D point, we can compute its projection onto each image. Now take the first image as the reference image. For each pixel of the first image, we assume a series of discrete depths (for how to determine the step for changing the depth see Appendix), and for each depth Z we compute the corresponding image points in the other 3 images.

$$[\tilde{x}_i^2(Z), \tilde{y}_i^2(Z)]^T = s_1 \mathbf{R}(1)^T [\tilde{x}_i^1, \tilde{y}_i^1, Z]^T \quad (31)$$
$$[\tilde{x}_i^3(Z), \tilde{y}_i^3(Z)]^T = s_2 \mathbf{R}(2)^T [\tilde{x}_i^1, \tilde{y}_i^1, Z]^T \quad (32)$$
$$[\tilde{x}_i^4(Z), \tilde{y}_i^4(Z)]^T = s_3 \mathbf{R}(3)^T [\tilde{x}_i^1, \tilde{y}_i^1, Z]^T \quad (33)$$

where $\mathbf{R}_{12}$, $\mathbf{R}_{13}$ and $\mathbf{R}_{14}$ are the first two rows of the rotation matrices between the first image and the second, third, fourth images, respectively. s_1, s_2, s_3 are the scale factors of the second, third and fourth images relative to the first image. In the case of orthographic projection, they are all 1.

To find the correct depth for each image point, we have two constraints: the linear geo-photometric constraint and the smoothness constraint. They are combined into a global energy functional,

$$
\begin{aligned}
E(Z) \;=\; & \sum_i (\tilde{a}_1 I_i^1(Z_i) + \tilde{a}_2 I_i^2(Z_i) + \tilde{a}_3 I_i^3(Z_i) \\
& + \; \tilde{a}_4 I_i^4(Z_i))^2 + \lambda \sum_i \sum_{k \in N_i} (Z_i - Z_k)^2 \;,(34)
\end{aligned}
$$

where λ is a scalar to balance the first term and the second term, N_i denotes the neighborhood of the i-th point in the first image. Our goal is to minimize the global energy of equation (34).

3.3 Optimization

We consider depth recovery as a labeling problem, where each label represents a depth value [8]. The depth takes some discrete values within a given range (see Appendix A for how to determine the depth step), and the number of depth values equals to the number of labels. A labeling problem usually takes the contextual information into consideration in an iterative fashion [8].

To optimize the global energy functional of (34), we could take a global optimization algorithm, such as simulated annealing, but its computation is very heavy [5]. In our approach, we employ a multiscale optimization algorithm introduced in [3]. The label configuration of the sites at the coarser level of the pyramid, as shown in Fig. 3, belongs to a constrained label space. Once the labels are determined at a coarser level, they are transfered to the finer level, and a new search is done around the labels determined at the coarser level. This algorithm was used to solve the motion estimation problem effectively [3]. We adapt the multiscale approach to our depth recovery problem.

Formally, we do the following sequence of optimizations:

$$
\tilde{Z}^l = \arg\min_{Z^l} E^l(Z^l) \tag{35}
$$

where Z^l represents the depth configuration at level l, E^l is the total energy at level l, and $\tilde{Z}^l$ is the estimate of the depth value, corresponding to the minimum energy at level l.

Each site at a coarser level corresponds to a block at the finer level. After the convergence at the coarser level, the points within the block inherit the same depth value from the coarser level. Intensity is always used in the original resolution, which avoids changing the intensity of the four images to different resolutions and storing them.

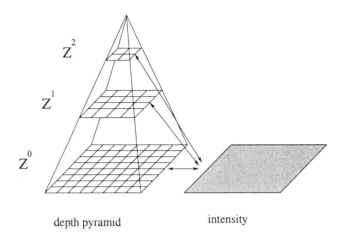

Figure 3. The optimization problem is solved gradually from the coarser level to the finer level in the pyramid.

At each level of the label pyramid, the simple algorithm ICM (Iterated Conditional Modes) is used to iterate search until convergence [2]. The convergence can be determined if the energy difference between two iterations is below a threshold, or the changes of Z are below a threshold. This is repeated from the coarsest level to the finest level. Finally, we obtain the depth map at the finest level or the original image.

4 Image Synthesis

In last section, we have shown how to recover depth for each pixel. Once the structure is reconstructed, we can synthesize new images using the recovered shape to determine the new position for each pixel and using the linear combination equation to determine the new intensity or color.

Given a new rotation $\mathbf{R}$ with respect to the reference image frame (in the current case the first image frame), and with the 3D shape known, we can compute the coordinates in the new image for each pixel in the reference image by

$$
[\tilde{x}_i(Z), \tilde{y}_i(Z)]^T = s\mathbf{R}^T [\tilde{x}_i^1, \tilde{y}_i^1, Z]^T \tag{36}
$$

where s is the scale of the new image relative to the reference image. In the case of orthographic projection, it is 1.

To compute the intensity for each pixel, we need to determine the coefficients first. We can generate 4 vectors by rotating an arbitrary unit vector, say, the horizontal axis by rotations $\mathbf{R}(1)$, $\mathbf{R}(2)$, $\mathbf{R}(3)$ and $\mathbf{R}$.

The coefficients can be computed by

$$\begin{bmatrix} a_1 \\ a_2 \\ a_3 \end{bmatrix} =$$

$$\left[\mathbf{R}(1) \begin{bmatrix} 1 \\ 0 \\ 0 \end{bmatrix} \ \mathbf{R}(2) \begin{bmatrix} 1 \\ 0 \\ 0 \end{bmatrix} \ \mathbf{R}(3) \begin{bmatrix} 1 \\ 0 \\ 0 \end{bmatrix} \right]^{-1} \mathbf{R} \begin{bmatrix} 1 \\ 0 \\ 0 \end{bmatrix} \ (37)$$

The intensity of the fourth image which is to be synthesized can be computed as a linear combination of the intensities of the other three images:

$$I_i = a_1 I_i^1 + a_2 I_i^2 + a_3 I_i^3 \qquad (38)$$

Since all computations are linear, synthesis is expected to be fast enough for realtime implementation.

5 Preliminary Experimental Results

We have done preliminary experiments on real face images. Implementation is yet to finish, and more improvements are due.

Fig.4 shows the original face images. They are taken by fixing the camera and the light sources while only moving the head.

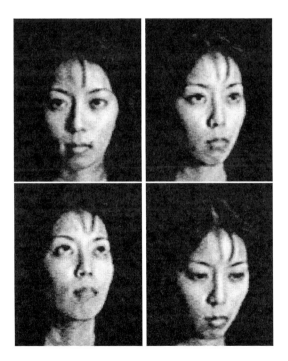

Figure 4. The original four images

We handpicked and matched a few feature points across the 4 images. And from them we computed

the rotations and scale changes relative to the first image (the front face image). Using the coordinates of these feature points, we computed the coefficients, and confirmed that the intensities of a few handpicked non-feature points do satisfy the same linear combination equation. After that, by minimizing (34), we reconstructed the structure, which is shown in Fig. 5. The depth is encoded as the brightness, the smaller the depth, the less brightness.

Figure 5. 3D reconstruction from the four images. The smaller the depth, the less brightness.

After the structure is recovered, we synthesized each image using the other three images. They are shown in Fig. 6, where we use an ellipse mask to elliminate the outside of the face, in order to focus our attention just on the face region, not the background. One can see that the synthesized images are very close to the original ones. This confirms that the intensity does satisfy the linear combination equation as well as the image coordinates. We did not use the linear combination equation to compute image coordinates. Instead we used the recovered depth map as a 3D surface and reprojected it onto new images.

To see further the image quality, we calculate the differences between the synthesized images and the original ones. And they are shown in Fig. 7. The difference is represented by the brightness, the smaller the difference, the less brightness. In fact, the difference is very small, so we scale the differences to the full intensity range (0-255) for display in Fig. 8. The fact that the difference between a real image and the synthesized image is so small suggests that object recognition can be done by examining the difference between the input intensity image and model intensity image rather than the edge maps.

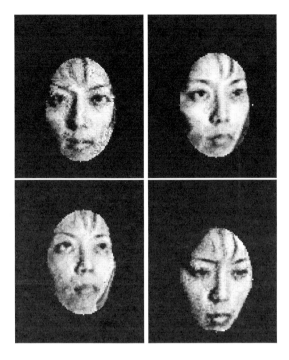

Figure 6. The synthesized four images

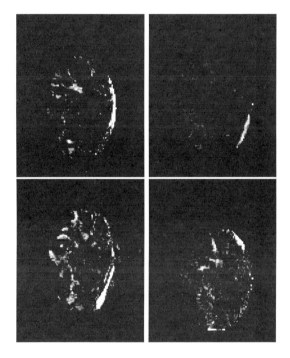

Figure 8. The differences between the four synthesized images and their corresponding original images are scaled to the full intensity range.

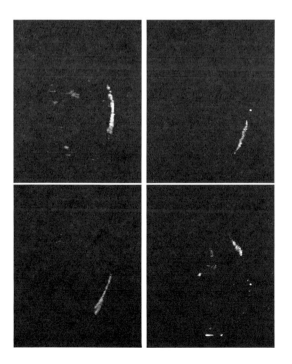

Figure 7. The differences between the four synthesized images and their corresponding original images

6 Conclusions

We have shown both theoretically and experimentally in this paper that both shape and shading share the same linear combination equation of the model images under the assumption that the orthographic or weak perspective camera and the light sources do not move while only the object moves. This is a quite general situation. We call this the *Linear Geo-Photometric Constraint*. This new constraint can be used for image matching, structure reconstruction, image synthesis and object recognition. Our preliminary experimental results show the feasibility of these applications.

7 Appendix   Determining the Depth Step ΔZ

The difference in position in the second image by changing depth from Z to $Z + \Delta Z$ is

$$\begin{bmatrix} \Delta x \\ \Delta y \end{bmatrix} = \mathbf{R}' \begin{bmatrix} 0 \\ 0 \\ \Delta Z \end{bmatrix} \qquad (39)$$

where $\mathbf{R}'$ is the first and second rows of the rotation matrix. For the difference to be 1 pixel long, we have

$$(R_{13}^2 + R_{23}^2)\Delta Z^2 = 1 \qquad (40)$$

where R_{13} and R_{23} denote the first row, third column component and second row, third column component of the rotation matices, respectively. Since we have 4 images, there are 3 depth steps computed,

$$\Delta Z^1 = \frac{1}{\sqrt{R_{13}(2)^2 + R_{23}(2)^2}} \qquad (41)$$

$$\Delta Z^2 = \frac{1}{\sqrt{R_{13}(3)^2 + R_{23}(3)^2}} \qquad (42)$$

$$\Delta Z^3 = \frac{1}{\sqrt{R_{13}(4)^2 + R_{23}(4)^2}}. \qquad (43)$$

We select the smallest one from the three as the step for changing depth.

References

[1] P. Belhumeur and D. Kriegman. What is the set of images of an object under all possible lighting conditions? In *CVPR*, pages 270–277, 1996.

[2] J. Besag. On the statistical analysis of dirty pictures. *Journal of the Royal Statistical Society, Series B*, 48:259–302, 1986.

[3] P. P. F. Heitz and P. Bouthemy. Multiscale minimization of global energy functions in some visual recovery problems. *CVGIP: Image Understanding*, 59(1):125–134, 1994.

[4] J. Foley, A. van Dam, S. Feiner, and J. Hughes. *Computer Graphics: Principles and Practice (2D Edition)*. Addison-Wesley Publishing Company, 1990.

[5] S. Geman and D. Geman. Stochastic relaxation, gibbs distribution and bayesian restoration of images. *IEEE Trans. PAMI*, 6:721–741, 1984.

[6] R. Hartley. Lines and points in three views. In *Proc of ARPA Image Understanding Workshop*, 1994.

[7] T. Huang and C. Lee. Motion and structure from orthographic projections. *IEEE Trans. PAMI*, 11:536–540, 1989.

[8] S. Li. *Markov Random Field Modeling in Computer Vision*. Springer-Verlag, New York, 1995.

[9] A. Maki, M. Watanabe, and C. Wiles. Geotensity: Combining motion and lighting for 3d surface reconstruction. In *Proc. Sixth Int'l Conf. Comput. Vision*, pages 1053–1060, 1998.

[10] L. Shapiro, A. Zisserman, and M. Brady. 3d motion recovery via affine epipolar geometry. *Int'l J. Comput. Vision*, 16:147–182, 1995.

[11] A. Shashua. *Geometry and Photometry in 3D Visual Recognition*. Ph.d dissertation, MIT, 1992.

[12] A. Shashua. Algebraic functions for recognition. *IEEE Trans. PAMI*, 17(8):779–789, Aug. 1995.

[13] C. Tomasi and T. Kanade. Shape and motion from image streams under orthography: a factorization method. *Int'l J. Comput. Vision*, 9(2):137–154, 1992.

[14] S. Ullman and R. Basri. Recognition by linear combinations of models. *IEEE Trans. PAMI*, 13(10):992–1106, 1991.

[15] G. Xu. A unified approach to image matching and segmentation in stereo, motion and object recognition via recovery of epipolar geometry. *VIDERE: A Journal of Computer Vision Research*, 1(1), Jan. 1997.

[16] G. Xu and N. Sugimoto. A linear algorithm for motion from three weak perspective images using euler angles. In *Proc. Third Asian Conf. Comput. Vision*, pages 543–550, 1998.

[17] G. Xu and N. Sugimoto. A linear algorithm for motion from three weak perspective images using euler angles. *IEEE Trans. PAMI*, 21(1):54–57, 1999.

[18] G. Xu and Z. Zhang. *Epipolar Geometry in Stereo, Motion and Object Recognition: A Unified Approach*. Kluwer Academic Publishers, 1996.

[19] Z. Zhang. Modeling geometric structure and illumination variation of a scene from real imgaes. In *Proc. Sixth Int'l Conf. Comput. Vision*, pages 1041–1046, Bombay, India, Jan. 1998.

Session IV

Image-Based Modeling—
Motion

Rendering Articulated Figures from Examples

Trevor Darrell

Interval Research, 1801C Page Mill Road, Palo Alto CA 94304

trevor@interval.com

Abstract

This paper presents new methods to robustly track and interpolate images of complex articulated figures. Traditional interpolation approaches fail on these cases since appearance is not necessarily a smooth function nor a linear manifold. We show how to model such appearance mappings with sets of examples which are each smooth functions. These well-behaved groups can cover overlapping regions of parameter space, and are empirically validated. A set growing procedure is used to find example clusters which are well-approximated within their convex hull; interpolation then proceeds only within a single such set. With this method physically valid images are produced even in regions of parameter space where the overall mapping is singular and nearby examples have different appearances. Our analysis stage tracks the occluding boundaries of articulated figures, even when there is no foreground contrast on an individual limb. Results generating both simulated and real arm images are demonstrated.

1 Introduction

To date, much attention has been given to the problem of view synthesis under varying camera pose or rigid object transformation. Several successful solutions have been proposed in the computer graphics and vision literature, including view morphing [14], plenoptic modeling/depth recovery [10], "lightfields" [9], and recent approaches using the trifocal tensor for view extrapolation [15].

For non-rigid view synthesis, networks for model-based interpolation and manifold learning have been used successfully in some cases [16, 3, 6, 13]. Techniques based on Radial Basis Function (RBF) interpolation or on Principle Components Analysis (PCA), have been able to interpolate face images under varying pose, expression and identity [1, 7, 8]. However, these methods are limited in the types of object appearance they can accurately model. PCA-based face analysis typically assumes images of face shape and texture fall in a linear subspace; RBF approaches fare poorly when appearance is not a smooth function.

We want to extend non-rigid interpolation networks to handle cases where appearance is not a linear manifold and is not a smooth function, such as with articulated bodies. The mapping from parameter to appearance for articulated bodies is often one-to-many due to the multiple solutions possible for a given endpoint. It will also be discontinuous when constraints call for different solutions across a boundary in parameter space, such as the example shown in Figure 1.

Our synthesis approach represents an appearance mapping as a set of piecewise smooth functions. We search for sets of examples which are well approximated by the examples on the convex hull of the set's parameter values. Once we have these 'safe' sets of examples we perform interpolation using only the examples in a single set.

The clear advantage of this approach is that it will prevent inconsistent examples from being combined during interpolation. It also can reduce the number of examples needed to fully interpolate the function, as only those examples which are on the convex hull of one or more example sets are needed. If a new example is provided and it falls within and is well-approximated by the convex hull of an existing set, it can be safely ignored.

Articulated bodies also often prove difficult for traditional optic-flow based methods for automatic correspondence estimation, a step which is critical for all image-based rendering algorithms. In the domain we have explored, images of limbs with uniform clothing or skin color create problems for tracking methods which require contrast to be present in the forground of an image feature. To overcome this problem we have formulated a contour tracker using a new robust image transform, and demonstrate how it can find the correspondences neccessary for rendering human figures in realistic imagery.

The remainder of this paper proceeds as follows. First, we will review synthesis methods for modeling appearance when it can be well approximated with a smooth and/or linear function. Next, we will present a technique for clustering examples to find maximal subsets which are well approximated in their interior, and will detail how we select among the subsets during interpolation. We will then present semi-automatic methods based on robust contour tracking for finding correspondence in images of human

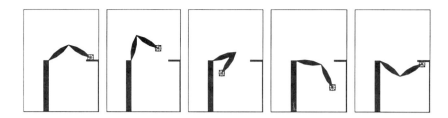

Figure 1: Synthesized examples of an appearance mapping (endpoint location to contour shape) for a 2DOF planar arm. Discontinuities in appearance due to workspace constraints make this a difficult function to learn from examples; the first and last example are very close in parameter space, but far in appearance space.

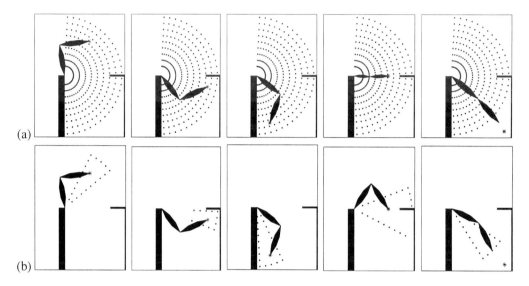

Figure 2: Arm appearance interpolated from examples using approximation network. (a) shows results using all examples in a single network; (b) using the example sets algorithm described in text. Note poor approximation on last two examples in (a); appearance discontinuities and extrapolation cause problems for full network, but are handled well in examples sets method.

arms with varying joint configuration. Finally, we will show the results of our manifold interpolation system on these arm images.

2 Modeling smooth and/or linear appearance functions

Traditional interpolation networks work well when object appearance can be modeled either as a linear manifold or as a smooth function over the parameters of interest (describing pose, expression, identity, configuration, etc.). As mentioned above, both PCA and RBF approaches have been successfully applied to model facial expression.

In both approaches, a key step in modeling non-rigid shape appearance from examples is to couple shape and texture into a single representation. Interpolation of shape has been well studied in the computer graphics literature (e.g., splines for key-frame animation) but does not alone render realistic images. PCA or RBF models of images

without a shape model can only represent and interpolate within a very limited range of pose or object configuration.

In a coupled representation, texture is modeled in shape-normalized coordinates, and shape is modeled as disparity between examples or displacement from a canonical example to all examples. Image warping is used to generate images for a particular texture and shape. Given a training set $\Omega = \{(y_i, x_i, d_i), 0 \leq i \leq n\}$, where y_i is the image of example i, x_i is the associated pose or configuration parameter, and d_i is a dense correspondence map relative to a canonical pose, a set of shape-aligned texture images can be computed such that texture t_i warped with displacement d_i renders example image y_i: $y_i = t_i \circ d_i$ [7, 1, 8]. A new image is constructed using a coupled shape model G and texture model F, based on input u:

$$\hat{y}(\Omega, u) = F_T(G_D(u), u) \, ,$$

where D, T are the matrices $[d_0 d_1 ... d_n]$, $[t_0 t_1 ... t_n]$, respec-

66

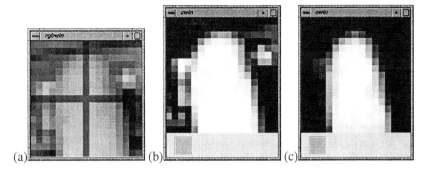

Figure 3: Construction of the Radial Cumulative Similarity (RCS) transform (From [4]). (a) Color window, (b) central color (in box at lower-left) and map of local similarity: bright pixels indicate similar value as central color. (c) RCS neighborhood image, computed by applying a radial propogation operator to the similarity image. This transform captures contrast of an occlusion boundary while ignoring background pixels.

tively.

In PCA-based approaches, G projects a portion of u onto a optimal linear subspace found from D, and F projects a portion of u onto a subspace found from T [8, 7]. For example $G_D(u) = P_D^m S_g u$, where S_g is a diagonal boolean matrix which selects the texture parameters from u and P_D^m is a matrix containing the m-th largest principle components of D. F warps the reconstructed texture according to the given shape: $F_T(u, s) = [P_T^m S_t u] \circ s$. While interpolation is simple using a PCA approach, the parameters used in PCA models often do not have any direct physical interpretation. For the task of view synthesis, an additional mapping $u = H(x)$ is needed to map from task parameters to PCA input values; a backpropagation neural net was used to perform this function for the task of eye gaze analysis [12].

Using the RBF-based approach [1], the application to view synthesis is straightforward. Both G and F are networks which compute locally-weighted regression, and parameters are used directly ($u = x$). G computes an interpolated shape, and F warps and blends the example texture images according to that shape: $G_D(x) = \sum_i c_i f(x - x_i)$, $F_T(x, s) = [\sum_i c_i' f(x - x_i)] \circ s$, where f is a radial basis function. The coefficients c and c' are derived from D and T, respectively: $C = DR^+$, where $r_{ij} = f(x_i - x_j)$ and C is the matrix of row vectors c_i; similarly $C' = TR^+$ [11]. We have found both vector norm and Gaussian basis functions give good results when appearance data is from a smooth function; the results below use $f(r) = ||r||$.

The method presented below for grouping examples into locally valid spaces is generally applicable to both the PCA and RBF-based view synthesis techniques. However our initial implementation, and the results reported in this paper, have been with RBF-based models.

3 Finding consistent example sets

Given examples from a complicated (non-linear, non-smooth) appearance mapping, we find local regions of appearance which are well-behaved as smooth, possibly linear, functions. We wish to cluster our examples into sets which can be used for successful interpolation using our local appearance model.

Conceptually, this problem is similar to that faced by Bregler and Omohundro [3], who built image manifolds using a mixture of local PCA models. Their work was limited to modeling shape (lip outlines); they used K-means clustering of image appearance to form the initial groupings for PCA analysis. However this approach had no model of texture and performed clustering using a mean-squared-error distance metric in simple appearance. Simple appearance clustering drastically over-partitions the appearance space compared to a model that jointly represent shape and texture. Examples which are distant in simple appearance can often be close when considered in 'vectorized' representation. Our work extends the notion of example clustering to the case of coupled shape and texture appearance models.

Our basic method is to find sets of examples which can be well-approximated from their convex hull in parameter space. We define a set growing criterion which enforces compactness and the good-interpolation property. To add a new point to an example set, we require both that the new point must be well approximated by the previous set alone and that all interior points in the resulting set be well interpolated from the exterior examples. We define exterior examples to be those on the convex hull of the set in parameter space. Given a training subset $s \subset \Omega$ and new point $p \in \Omega$,

$$E(s, p) = \max(E_I(s \cup \{p\}), E_E(s, p)) ,$$

67

Figure 4: (a) Images of a real arm (from a sequence of 33 images) with changing appearance and elbow configuration. (b) First frame in a image pair from this sequence where the user moves his arm. 9 feature locations are marked. (c) Results of feature tracking in second frame with RCS-based norm. (d) Results with least-squares norm. See following figure for detail.

with the interior error

$$E_I(s) = \max_{p' \in (s - \mathcal{H}_x(s))} ||y_{p'} - \hat{y}(\mathcal{H}_x(s), x_{p'})|| \, ,$$

and the extrapolation error

$$E_E(s, p) = ||y_p - \hat{y}(\mathcal{H}_x(s), x_p)|| \, .$$

$\mathcal{H}_x(s)$ is the subset of s whose x vectors lie on the convex hull of all such vectors in s. To add a new point, we require $E < \epsilon$, where ϵ is a free parameter of the clustering method.

Given a seed example set, we look to nearest neighbors in appearance space to find the next candidate to add. Unless we are willing to test the extrapolation error of the current model to all points, we have to rely on precomputed non-vectorized appearance distance (e.g., MSE between example images). If the examples are sparse in the appearance domain, this may not lead to effective groupings.

If examples are provided in sequence and are based on observations from an object with realistic dynamics, then we can find effective groupings even if observations are sparse in appearance space. We make the assumption that along the trajectory of example observations over time, the underlying object is likely to remain smooth and locally span regions of appearance which are possible to interpolate. We thus perform set growing along examples on their input trajectory. Specifically, in the results reported below, we select K seed points on the trajectory to form initial clusters. At each point p we find the set s which is

the smallest interval on the example trajectory which contains p, has a non-zero interior region $(s - \mathcal{H}_x(s))$, and for which $E_I(s) < \epsilon$. If such set exists, we continue to expand it, growing the set along the example trajectory until the above set growing criterion is violated. Once we can no longer grow any set, we test whether any set is a proper subset of another, and delete it if so. We keep the remaining sets, and use them for interpolation as described below.

4   Synthesis using example sets

We generate new views using sets of examples: interpolation is restricted to only occur inside the convex hull of an example set found as above for which $E_I(s) \leq \epsilon$. Given a new parameter vector x, we test whether it is in the convex hull of parameters in any example set. If the point does not lie in the convex hull of any example set, we find the nearest point on the convex hull of one of the example sets, and use that instead. This prevents erroneous extrapolation.

If a new parameter is in the convex hull of more than one example set, we first select the set whose median example parameter is closest to the desired example parameter. Once a set has been selected, we interpolate a new function value from examples using the RBF method summarized above. To enforce temporal consistency of rendered images over time, we can use a simple additional constraint on subsequent frames. Once we have selected an example set, we keep using it until the desired parameter value leaves the valid region (convex hull) of that set. When this occurs, we allow transitions only to "adjacent" example sets; adjacency is defined as those pairs of sets for

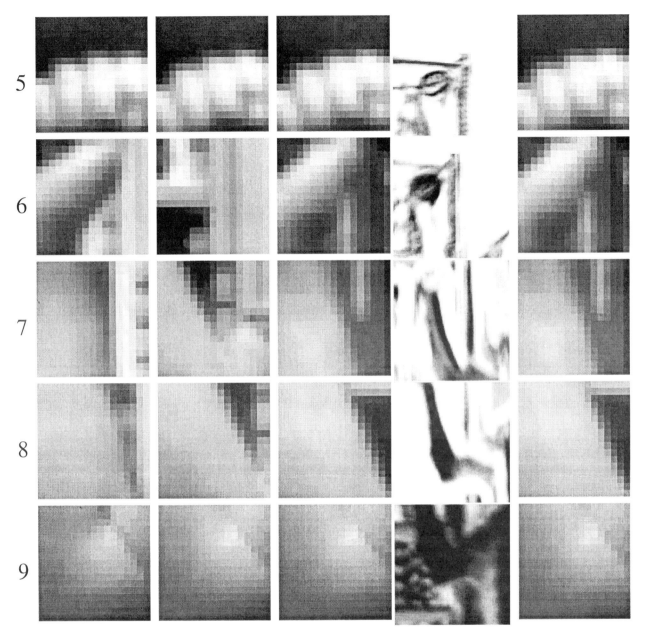

Figure 5: Detail of tracked features 5-9 in previous figure. Each row shows results for different feature location number. First column shows image window in first image. Second column shows image window in second image corresponding to optimal displacement found using L2 norm. Third column shows result using anisotropically smoothed RCS norm. Fourth column shows RCS distance function for all displacement values. Fifth column shows final result, after residual error test on L2 norm.

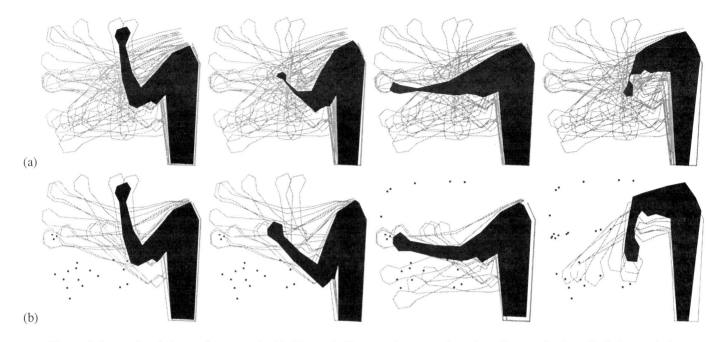

(a)

(b)

Figure 6: Interpolated shape of arms tracked in Figure 4. Top row shows results using all examples in a single interpolation network; bottom row shows results using example sets algorithm. Open contours show arms example locations; filled contour shows interpolation result. Near regions of appearance singularity in parameter space the full network method generates physically-invalid arm shapes; the example sets method produces realistic images.

which at least one example on each convex hull are sufficiently close ($\|y_i - y_j\| < \epsilon$) in appearance space.

5 Tracking articulated limbs

A key input to example-based image synthesis methods which operate on natural images is accurate image disparity, or correspondence. For each point on each example image, we need to compute the equivalent location in a cannonical reference frame, yielding the matrix D used in Section 2. To apply our method to real imagery, such as the arm sequence in Figure 4(a), we need a method to track the arm as it moves through the scene. This feature tracking and/or "optic flow" computation is a classic problem in computer vision.

Unfortunately, articulated figures pose a particular problem for existing solutions to local feature tracking. When a figure has multiple moving segments and thus many occluding boundaries, it must have considerable contrast on each segment for conventional tracking techniques to succeed. (This includes the robust redecending norms pioneered in [2], which can discount outliers but fail when there is no foreground contrast.) Often this is not the case, such as when segments are in fact skin or cloth of a uniform color.

Recently, we have developed a new robust image transform that can be used to track occluding contours accurately. As reported in [4], a local representation of the

shape of image attribute homogeneity is a stable feature at occluding boundaries. We call this representation Radial Cumulative Similarity (RCS), since it is computed by radially integrating the similarity of points in the window relative to the center. Figure 3 illustrates the computation of the RCS transform of an image window containing a fingertip.

To track the arm in the sequence shown in Figure 4(a), we used an interactive contour tracing system based on RCS feature tracking. A cannonical contour was traced in the initial frame, and key points along that contour tracked automatically in subsequent frames. When errors occured, they were edited by the operator. Figure 4(b-d) shows the automatic tracking process for various features on one limb, using both RCS and conventional least-squares based tracking. Figure 5 shows the detail on several tracked features; unlike conventional approaches at these points the RCS-based method is able to follow an occluding contour of the limb where little or no foreground contrast is present.

6 Synthesis Results

First we show examples using a synthetic arm with several workspace constraints. Figure 1 shows examples of a simple planar 2DOF arm and the inverse kinematic solution for a variety of endpoints. Due to an artificial obstacle in the world, the arm is forced to switch between arm-up and arm-down configurations to avoid collision.

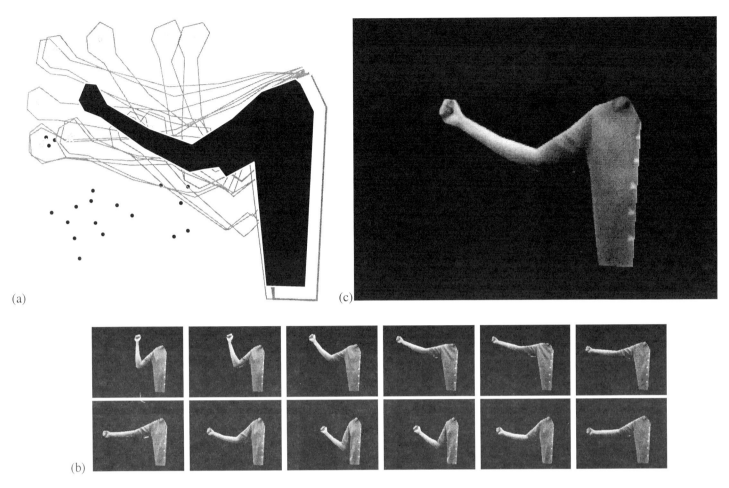

(a)

(c)

(b)

Figure 7: Interpolated shape and texture result. (a) shows exemplar contours (open) and interpolated shape (filled). (b) shows example texture images. (c) shows final interpolated image.

We used RBF interpolation to model the appearance of the arm as a function of endpoint location. Appearance was modeled as the vector of contour point locations, in this case obtained from the synthetic arm rendering function. We first trained a single RBF network on a dense set of examples of this appearance function. Figure 2(a) shows results interpolating new arm images from these examples; results are accurate except where there are regions of appearance discontinuity due to workspace constraints, or when the network extrapolates erroneously.

We applied our clustering method described above to this data, yielding the results shown in Figure 2(b). None of the problems with discontinuities or erroneous extrapolation can be seen in these results, since our method enforces the constraint that an interpolated result must be returned from on or within the convex hull of a valid example set.

Next we applied our method to the images of real arms shown in Figure 4, using the tracking method outlined

above. Figure 6(a) shows interpolated arm shapes using a single RBF on all examples; dramatic errors can be seen near where multiple different appearances exist within a small region of parameter space.

Figure 6(b) shows the results on the same points using sets of examples found using our clustering method; physically realistic arms are generated in each case. Figure 7 shows the final interpolated result rendered with both shape and texture.

7 Conclusions and Future Work

View-based image interpolation is a powerful paradigm for generating realistic imagery without full models of the underlying scene geometry. Current techniques for non-rigid interpolation assume appearance is a smooth function. Using example clustering and on-line cross validation, one can decompose a complex appearance mapping into sets of examples which can be smoothly interpolated. We showed results on real imagery of human arms, using robust contour tracking. Given images of an arm moving on a plane with various configuration conditions (elbow up and elbow down), and with associated parameter vectors marking the hand location, our method is able to discover a small set of manifolds with a small number of exemplars each can render new examples which are always physically correct. A single interpolating manifold for this same data has errors near the boundary between different arm configurations, and where multiple images have the same parameter value.

There are three main limitations in our present system, which we are working to improve upon. First, rather than track each feature location independently, we can augment our contour tracking system to incorporate "snake"-like internal energy terms. This can dramatically reduce errors due to the aperture problem. Initial results with RCS-based dynamic contour tracking can be found in [5]; we are currently adding this functionality to our articulated tracking system. Second, to perform image synthesis we need dense correspondences, which for the results above we interpolate from tracked values on the contour. This is suboptimal, since there may well be contrast and/or shape deformations in the interior. Rather than perform contour tracking, an explicitly computed dense correspondence map is the ultimate goal to which we are working. Finally, the use of a single cannonical shape coordinate frame, while mathematically elegant for the synthesis phase, places a severe burden on the tracking system. In a future version this assumption will be relaxed, with a separate coordinate systems for each distinct example cluster.

8 Acknowledgments

The author would like to thank Michele Covell and Aaron Hertzmann for help with visual tracking and rendering code.

References

[1] D. Beymer, A. Shashua and T. Poggio, Example Based Image Analysis and Synthesis, MIT AI Lab Memo No. 1431, MIT, 1993. also see D. Beymer and T. Poggio, *Science* 272:1905-1909, 1996.

[2] M. Black and P. Anandan, A framework for robust estimation of optical flow, 4th Proc. ICCV, 1993.

[3] C. Bregler and S. Omohundro, Nonlinear Image Interpolation using Manifold Learning, NIPS-7, MIT Press, 1995.

[4] T. Darrell, A Radial Cumulative Similarity Transform for Robust Image Correspondence, Proc. CVPR-98, Santa Barbara, CA, IEEE CS Press, 1998.

[5] M. Covell and T. Darrell, Dynamic Occluding Contours: A new external energy term for snakes, Submitted CVPR-99.

[6] M. Jagersand, Image Based View Synthesis of Articulated Agents, Proc. CVPR-97, San Jaun, Pureto Rico, pp. 1047-1053, IEEE CS Press, 1997.

[7] M. Jones and T. Poggio, Multidimensional Morphable Models, Proc. ICCV-98, Bombay, India, pp. 683-688, 1998.

[8] A. Lanitis, C.J. Taylor, T.F. Cootes, A Unified Approach to Coding and Interpreting Face Images, Proc. ICCV-95, pp. 368-373, Cambridge, MA, 1995.

[9] M. Levoy and P. Hanrahan, Light Field Rendering, In SIGGRAPH-96, pp. 31-42, 1996.

[10] L. McMillan and G. Bishop, Plenoptic Modeling: An image-based rendering system. In Proc. SIGGRAPH-95, pp. 39-46, 1995.

[11] T. Poggio and F. Girosi, A Theory of Networks for Approximation and Learning, MIT AI Lab Memo No. 1140. 1989.

[12] T. Rikert and M. Jones, Gaze Estimation using Morphable Models, Proc. IEEE Conf. Face and Gesture Recognition '98, pp. 436-441, Nara, Japan, IEEE CS Press, 1998.

[13] L. Saul and M. Jordan, A Variational Principle for Model-based Morphing, NIPS-9, MIT Press, 1997.

[14] S. Seitz and C. Dyer, View Morphing, in Proc. SIGGRAPH-96, pp. 21-30, 1996.

[15] A. Shashua and M. Werman, Trilinearity of Three Perspective Views and its Associated Tensor, in Proc. ICCV-95, pp. 920-935, Cambridge, MA, IEEE CS Press, 1995.

[16] J. Tenenbaum, Mapping a manifold of perceptual observations, NIPS-10, MIT Press, 1998.

Synthesis and recognition of biological motion patterns based on linear superposition of prototypical motion sequences

M. A. Giese and T. Poggio
Center for Biological and Computational Learning
Massachusetts Institute of Technology, E25-206 / 218
Cambridge, MA 02142, USA

Abstract

The linear-combination of prototypical views has been shown to provide a powerful method for the recognition and analysis of images of three-dimensional stationary objects. In this paper, we present preliminary results on an extension of this idea to video sequences. For this extension, the computation of correspondences in space-time turns out to be the central theoretical problem, which we solve with a new correspondence algorithm. Using simulated images of biological motion we demonstrate the usefulness of the superposition of prototypical sequences for the synthesis of new video sequences, and for the analysis and recognition of actions.

Our method permits to impose a topology over the space of video sequences of action patterns. This topology is more complicated than a linear space. We present a new method that is based on the structural risk minimization principle of statistical learning theory, which permits to exploit this knowledge about the topology of the pattern space for recognition.

1 Introduction

The two-dimensional views of three-dimensional objects change continuously with the orientation of the object in space. This permits to represent intermediate views of an object by interpolation between prototypical views. This idea has been extensively exploited by Vetter and Poggio [14] who demonstrated that it is possible to define linear spaces over sets of views of the same three-dimensional object. For this purpose, the correspondence vector fields that result from the calculation of the correspondences between a set of prototypical views of the object, and a reference image, were used as basis vectors of a linear vector space. Such correspondence vector fields can be linearly superpositioned, resulting in a smooth morphing between the different prototypical views of the object. This permits to represent a whole class of similar images of an object in a very compact way through the weights of this linear superposition. Since correspondences can be calculated also between images of slightly different objects, e.g. faces of two different individuals, the same technique permits to morph between different faces. Additionally, complex image transformations, like a change of the pose of an object, can be represented as a nonlinear transformation in the space of the weights. Such mappings can be represented with radial basis function networks, and can be learned from a set of example images [1].

The linear combination of prototypical views has been successfully applied to a number of different problems, like the view-invariant recognition of faces [1], for view morphing [7], and for the generation of animation sequences [5]. The underlying strategy has been also generalized to three-dimensional images [13].

These promising results from the application of linear object classes to stationary images has motivated us to investigate if similar ideas can be transferred to the the recognition and synthesis of motion patterns, or actions in video sequences. If it would be possible to represent image sequences by adequately defined linear superpositions of prototypical sequences, the advantages of the linear combination of prototypes could potentially transferred to the recognition an synthesis of movements patterns and actions. It is the aim of this paper to give a first evaluation of this new concept in the context of a simple example. We analyzed the synthesis and the analysis of motion patterns using simulated images of biological motion.

We believe that the proposed method provides a new interesting alternative to existing methods for action recognition, that are usually either model-based (e.g. [10, 4, 15]), or relying on the extraction of adequate spatio-temporal features (e.g. [9, 4, 3]). We assume that our method is also interesting for computer graphics applications since it permits to morph between different actions or movements.

2 Linear object classes for stationary images

To set up a framework that will be helpful for the discussion of the theoretical problems that are associated with the generalization of the concept of linear object classes to image sequences, we start with a short review of the ideas of Vetter and Poggio [14].

How can an image be represented by a linear superposition of a set prototypical example images? The linear combination of the brightness values of images on a pixel-by-pixel basis provides no useful definition for such a superposition. The superposition of the images would look like two transparent objects. Only when the the shapes of the two-dimensional projections of the object in the images are exactly the same the superposition would only look natural.

A more useful definition for the linear combination of prototypical images is based on the correspondences between the images. Assume that the image features, e.g. the pixels, are characterized by a vector $\mathbf{x}$, and that a reference image is chosen that is characterized by the vector $\mathbf{x}_0$. The image can then be characterized by a correspondence vector $\boldsymbol{\xi} = \mathbf{x} - \mathbf{x}_0$ that describes the spatial shifts between corresponding points of the image and the reference image. Such correspondence vectors can be calculated with a usual optic flow algorithm.

Given a set of prototypical images that are characterized by the feature vectors $\mathbf{x}_p$, and by the correspondence vectors $\boldsymbol{\xi}_p$ with respect to the reference image $\mathbf{x}_0$, one can define a nicely interpolating linear combination of images by linearly combining the spatial shift vectors $\boldsymbol{\xi}_p$ in the form:

$$\boldsymbol{\xi} = \sum_{p=1}^{P} c_p \, \boldsymbol{\xi}_p \qquad (1)$$

The constants c_p determine the contributions of the individual prototypical images. From the obtained new correspondence vector $\boldsymbol{\xi}$ a new image feature vector $\mathbf{x}$ can be calculated, just by adding the shift vector to the reference vector: $\mathbf{x} = \boldsymbol{\xi} + \mathbf{x}_0$. This is a warping of the reference image that is specified by the new correspondence vector $\boldsymbol{\xi}$. By applying this method the topology of a linear space is defined onto the set of images. Of course, the prototypical images and the represented image must be sufficiently similar, so that an interpolation between the prototypes makes sense.

The defined linear space of images can be used for the synthesis of new images, and for analysis or recognition. For synthesis prototypical images from different objects, e.g. faces from different persons or

view angles are linearly combined. This leads to a smooth morphing between the prototypical images. New images can be characterized by the relatively low-dimensional coefficient vector $\mathbf{c} = [c_1, c_2, ..., c_P]'$. Complex image transformations, like rotations of a three-dimensional object, can be expressed by the associated changes of the coefficient vector $\mathbf{c}$. Transformations of the image space correspond to the application of nonlinear mappings on the coefficient vector $\mathbf{c}$. Such mappings can be represented by radial basis function networks [11], that can be trained with a set of example images for which the true transformation is known [1].

For analysis, the correspondence between a new image and the reference image is calculated. The resulting correspondence vector $\boldsymbol{\xi}$ is then approximated by a linear combination of the prototypical correspondence vectors $\boldsymbol{\xi}_p$, e.g. by least squares fitting. The resulting coefficient vectors can be used to estimate the pose parameters of three-dimensional objects. For this purpose, a radial basis function network is trained with image examples that represents the mapping from the coefficient vector $\mathbf{c}$ onto the pose parameters [1].

3 Linear object classes for image sequences

To transfer the idea of a linear combination of prototypes to whole image or video sequences one might first think about a relatively simple solution. The correspondences between the image sequences could be defined by calculating the correspondences between the images for each fixed point in time on a frame-by-frame basis. The linear combination of the prototypical sequences would then be defined simply by a "time-indexed" version of equation (1):

$$\boldsymbol{\xi}(t) = \sum_{p=1}^{P} c_p \, \boldsymbol{\xi}_p(t)$$

The disadvantage of this simple procedure is that image sequences with identical spatial structure, but slightly different timing result in large spatial deviation vectors, almost like two sequences that show different movements. Assume that two video sequences show the same arm movement of two different persons, one of which moves his arm faster in the beginning, and slower at the end of the movement than the other. If only spatial displacements enter the correspondence process, these two image sequences would be matched with very strong spatial displacements between the corresponding image points. A linear combination of prototypes with such large spatial displacement vectors would likely lead to distortions that prevent a smooth interpolation between the arm movements of the two persons.

A useful definition for the "linear combination" of image sequences must, therefore, result in a good interpolation between sequences with slightly different temporal structure. To interpolate smoothly between sequences with similar spatial, but different temporal structure we must admit also *shifts in time* between the corresponding image points in the sequences. This implies that we must calculate *spatio-temporal correspondences*.

These considerations lead to the idea to define not only a spatial displacement vector $\boldsymbol{\xi}(t)$, but also a temporal displacement parameter $\tau(t)$ for each point in time. Instead of the linear superposition equation (1) one obtains the pair of equations:

$$\boldsymbol{\xi}(t) = \sum_{p=1}^{P} c_p \, \boldsymbol{\xi}_p(t) \qquad (2)$$

$$\tau(t) = \sum_{p=1}^{P} c_p \, \tau_p(t)$$

Each correspondence vector has thus a spatial and a temporal component, which are linearly combined using the same weighting coefficients. In the rest of this article, we demonstrate that this definition of a linear combination of image sequences leads to useful results.

4   Correspondences in space-time

We have, so far, not specified how spatio-temporal correspondences image sequences can be calculated. The spatio-temporal correspondence algorithm must assign to each spatial point in the feature space at a certain point in time in one image sequence a, usually spatially and temporally shifted point in the another sequence.

It is important to understand that finding spatio-temporal correspondences is an *ill-posed problem*. Assume for a moment that the feature space is only one dimensional. In this case the image sequences can be characterized by two one-dimensional time functions $x_1(t)$ and $x_2(t)$. Assume now, that the two functions specify two movements that have exactly the same spatial structure, but which have a different timing. Let, for instance, the movement of the trajectory x_2 first be slower, and then faster than the movement of x_1. In this case we could assign a whole continuum of

spatio-temporal shifts that map the two curves continuously onto each other. We could for instance try to minimize the temporal shifts and assign $\tau(t) = 0$ to each point in time. The deviations between the two functions would then be captured by the spatial shifts. If one, however, favors the other extreme, and imposes no restrictions on the temporal shifts at all, one can obtain zero spatial shifts everywhere just by rewarping the trajectory x_1 onto the other trajectory in time. (Since we assumed that the two trajectories have the same spatial structure this is always possible.) From this can be concluded that a unique solution for the spatio-temporal correspondence problem requires the inclusion of a priori information about the trade-off between temporal and spatial shifts. This trade-off determines the regimes over which the obtained representation interpolates in space and time.

We have developed a correspondence algorithm that resolves this ambiguity. The algorithm should assign to each point $\mathbf{x}_2(t)$ on the trajectory $\mathbf{x}_2$ a corresponding point on the trajectory $\mathbf{x}_1$, which not necessarily has the same time value. We introduce, therefore the modified time t'. The pair of corresponding point to time t is thus given by the points $\mathbf{x}_2(t)$ and $\mathbf{x}_1(t')$. The corresponding points can also be uniquely characterized by their spatial and temporal shifts that are indexed by the continuous time parameter t. Mathematically, these shifts are defined by the equations:

$$\mathbf{x}_2(t) = \mathbf{x}_1(t') + \boldsymbol{\xi}(t) \qquad (3)$$

$$t' = t + \tau(t)$$

Our correspondence algorithm determines the temporal and spatial shifts by minimizing an error that is the weighted sum of the quadratic spatial and temporal deviations over the whole image sequence. In the time-continuous case, this error is given by the integral:

$$E_c[\boldsymbol{\xi}, \tau] = \int \left[|\boldsymbol{\xi}(t)|^2 + \lambda \, \tau(t)^2 \right] \mathrm{d}t \qquad (4)$$

This error is a functional of the spatial displacement function $\boldsymbol{\xi}(t)$, and of the temporal displacement function $\tau(t)$. The error has to be minimized under the additional constraint that the mapping between the time variable t and the modified time t' for the trajectory $\mathbf{x}_1(t')$ must be continuous, one-to-one, and monotonically increasing, in order to define unique temporal warping of the sequence $\mathbf{x}_1$. This implies for the function $\tau(t)$ the following constraints:

$$\mathrm{d}\tau/\mathrm{d}t > -1 \qquad (5)$$

$$\tau(0) = \tau(t_{\max}) = 0 \qquad (6)$$

For the minimization of the error E_c, we have developed an algorithm that combines dynamic programming and parametric optimization. (The technical details are discussed in appendix A.)

5 Application for the synthesis of new image sequences

To test the appropriateness of our idea of a linear combination of prototypical image sequences, we generated a set of synthetic image sequences that showed a stick figure that performs three different walking styles (walking, running and limping). Using a 3D-model for the stick figure, we generated for each of the three walking styles two-dimensional image sequences from five different view angles (one view was directly from the side; for the additionally views, the "camera" axis was rotated either ± 25 deg up and down, or 25 deg right or left. The prototype for "limping" was obtained from the image sequence for "walking" by rewarping the image sequence for walking in time, by first slowing the movement down, and then increasing its speed in order to keep the cycle time of the movement constant.) In total, we used 15 different prototypical sequences (five different view angles for each of the three walking styles), each sampled with only 21 discrete time steps.

We used the two-dimensional joint positions of the figure as feature vectors $\mathbf{x}(t)$. The algorithm described above was applied for the calculation of the correspondences between the prototypical patterns and a reference sequence, which was the side view of walking. The obtained spatio-temporal correspondence fields of the prototypes were then linearly combined according to equation (2) using weights that fulfilled the conditions $c_p \geq 0$ and

$$\sum_{p=1}^{P} c_p = 1.$$

The resulting new correspondence vector field was then used to warp the reference sequence $\mathbf{x}_1(t)$ to a new synthetic sequence that is defined by the equation:

$$\mathbf{x}(t) = \mathbf{x}_1(t + \tau(t)) + \boldsymbol{\xi}(t) \qquad (7)$$

Our tests showed that the synthesized new image sequences interpolated smoothly between the prototypical sequences of the *same* walking style. The quality of the resulting interpolated motion sequences was comparable to the quality of the prototypical sequences themselves. Interestingly, also linear combinations of *different* walking styles looked relatively

natural, as long as the view angles were similar. A combination of "walking" and "running" with equal weights looks like slow running or quick walking. A mixture of "limping" and "running" looks like a weak form of limping. This shows that, at least with the stick figures, the proposed method permits to interpolate smoothly between different views of a single walking style, and also between different action pattern. In particular, the smooth interpolation between walking and limping, that differed only with respect to their temporal structure, shows that the method fulfills the constraint that was formulated above: it interpolates smoothly between patterns that differ with respect to their temporal structure.

When two different walking styles with different view angles were combined the resulting motion sequences showed distortions. This shows that not all motion patters can be linearly combined equally well. The combination of some patterns, like prototypes of the same walking style, or different walking styles with the same viewing parameters, leads to useful interpolated patterns. Combinations of prototypes that differ in both, view angle and walking style seem not to form useful linear combinations. More abstractly, this can be interpreted as evidence for the existence of a topology over the set of image sequences. In this topology, some prototypical patterns seem to be close, like prototypes for the same walking style, or different walking styles with the same view parameters, and an interpolation between them led therefore to useful results. Other sequences, like running and limping from different view angles seem to further apart, so that an interpolation between them leads not to useful results. Interestingly, the mixture of all prototypical patterns with equal weights leads to a natural pattern, potentially because the characteristic extreme properties of the different prototypes are averaged out. We are presently investigating if similar results can also be obtained with real image sequences.

6 Analysis of image sequences

To test if the linear combination of prototypical sequences can also be used for the recognition of walking styles and their view parameters, we simulated new synthetic image sequences that showed the walking styles from many different view angles. We tried to recover the walking style, and the view parameters (rotation angles of the camera).

Let us assume first that the walking style is already known. In this case the view parameters can be recovered by approximating the spatial and temporal shifts

$\boldsymbol{\xi}(t)$ and $\tau(t)$, that are associated with the new sequence, by a linear combination of the shifts of the prototypical sequences of this walking style, according to equation (2). This can be easily achieved by minimizing a composite error that is a weighted sum of the squared errors of the spatial and the temporal deviations of the approximation:

$$E_a(\mathbf{c}) = \int \left[|\boldsymbol{\xi}(t) - \sum_{p=1}^{P} c_p \boldsymbol{\xi}_p(t)|^2 + \right.$$
$$\left. \lambda_a \left(\tau(t) - \sum_{p=1}^{P} c_p \tau(t) \right)^2 \right] \, \mathrm{d}t \quad (8)$$

The parameter λ_a determines the trade-off between spatial and temporal deviations. The coefficient vector $\mathbf{c}$ that minimizes the error E_a can be found by solving the linear equation system

$$\mathbf{K}\,\mathbf{c} = \mathbf{a} \quad (9)$$

where the elements of the $P \times P$ matrix $\mathbf{K}$ are given by

$$K_{pq} = \int \left[\boldsymbol{\xi}_p(t)' \boldsymbol{\xi}_q(t) + \lambda_a \, \tau_p(t) \tau_q(t) \right] \, \mathrm{d}t \quad (10)$$

and the elements of the vector $\mathbf{a}$ by

$$a_p = \int \left[\boldsymbol{\xi}(t)' \boldsymbol{\xi}_p(t) + \lambda_a \, \tau(t) \tau_p(t) \right] \, \mathrm{d}t \quad (11)$$

for $1 \leq p, q \leq P$. This equation system was solved using a singular value decomposition method. The coefficient vectors were then used as input signals for a radial basis function network with gaussian basis functions that maps the coefficient vectors onto the view angles. This network had been trained with 16 image sequences with known pose parameters. The width of the gaussian basis functions was optimized for good interpolation properties of the networks. The view angles were recovered with a precision of about 2 deg in the regime ± 25 deg for both viewing angles by this procedure.

Recovering the type of the walking style from the weights of the linear combination turned out to be more difficult. The reason for that is that an application of usual least squares techniques for the estimation of the view parameters fails when prototypes from all different walking styles are used at the same time. The reason is the high ambiguity in the possibility to decompose the new correspondence vector in linear combinations of the correspondence vectors of the prototypes. This results in coefficient vectors that load highly on many different walking patterns, and also on combinations of coefficients that do not specify useful linear combinations of the prototypes (for instance "running" and "limping" from different view angles). This is illustrated in Fig. 1 (left), where the gray levels encode the absolute values of the coefficients c_p. Along the vertical axis of this plots the coefficient vector elements are ordered according to the walking style of the associated prototype (W: walking, R: running, L: limping). Each segment on the horizontal axis indicates one of 48 test sequences that had to be classified as one of the three different walking styles. The left figure shows the results that are obtained using a least squares method for the estimation of the coefficients. Examples for a certain walking style, like "running", lead to substantial load on the coefficients also of other walking styles, like "limping". This unstable estimation makes a reliable recognition of the walking style from the weights impossible. This is true even though we applied singular value decomposition and regularization techniques in order to stabilize solution of the least squares estimation problem.

The deeper mathematical reason for this instability is that the set of prototypical correspondence vectors defines linear function set for approximation that is too rich (its *capacity* is too large). The resulting instability in the estimation of the coefficients could potentially be resolved by adding more features, that could help to disambiguate the linear estimation problem. We will take another route here that exploits the knowledge that we have about the topology of the space of image sequences. It seems reasonable to require that prototypes that do not specify usefully interpolating intermediate patterns if they are superpositioned, should not contribute at the same time to the linear approximation. This helps to avoid that the motion pattern is approximated by linear combinations that do not correspond to usefully interpretable image sequences.

How can this a priori knowledge be integrated in the estimation of the coefficient vector $\mathbf{c}$? We propose here a numerical technique that is based on the *structural risk minimization (SRM)* principle that has been formulated by Vapnik [12]. The idea of structural risk minimization is to look for a solution with minimal capacity of the associated function set, instead of minimizing only the approximation error in the least squares estimation in (9). We propose here to embed the a priori knowledge into the capacity control, resulting a *modified structural risk minimization* (MSRM) method. To measure the capacity we use the

77

function:

$$E_s(\mathbf{c}) = |\mathbf{c}|'\mathbf{W}|\mathbf{c}| \qquad (12)$$

When $\mathbf{W}$ is the unit matrix, this function goes over in the function that is usually applied for structural risk minimization, which results in a solution that minimizes the VC dimension [12]. We modified this term by admitting additional positive values in the symmetric matrix $\mathbf{W}$. All elements that correspond to pairs of coefficients that specify meaningless combinations of prototypes were set to high positive values. This leads to a strong suppression of such weight combinations in the solution.

The function E_s has to be minimized under the constraint $\mathbf{K}\,\mathbf{c} = \mathbf{a}$. In practice, this constraint can be often only approximately fulfilled, because of noise and inconsistencies in the data. This makes it necessary to induce a "slack variable" vector $\boldsymbol{\zeta}$ into the problem that absorbs the deviations from the equality constraint. Instead of the function in (12) we minimize thus the expression

$$\tilde{E}_s(\mathbf{c}) = |\mathbf{c}|'\mathbf{W}|\mathbf{c}| + C\,|\boldsymbol{\zeta}|^2 \qquad (13)$$

under the constraint $\mathbf{A}\mathbf{c} = \mathbf{a} + \boldsymbol{\zeta}$. The large positive constant C determines how strongly deviations from the equality constraints are punished in the optimization process. It is shown in appendix B that this optimization problem can be transformed into a quadratic programming problem for which effective solution algorithms exist.

Fig. 1 (right) shows that our MSRM method leads to approximations with relatively few non-zero coefficients that are usually corresponding to prototypes of the true walking pattern. This makes it possible to use the linear weights for a classification of the walking patterns. We used the L_1-norm of the parts of the coefficient vector that belong to the individual walking styles as discriminating function for the classification. For the tested 48 examples the misclassification rate using the MSRM method for the estimation of the coefficients was low ($< 5\%$). Applying the same classification rule to the coefficient vectors that were obtained using least squares fitting lead to very high error rates of the classification (about 30%). This shows that the increased numerical effort that is required for the solution of the quadratic programming problem is justified.

A very interesting result was obtained when a new walking pattern was generated between walking and running, by adequately mixing the coefficients of the 3D-simulation program. In this situation the relative size of the L_1-norms of the coefficient vectors associated with running and walking prototypes covaried exactly with the relative influence of the two walking styles in the simulation program. This shows that our method permits a gradual classification of action patterns that permits results of the form: x % "walking" or "running". The method performs thus a mixture between classification and parametric regression.

Fig. 1:

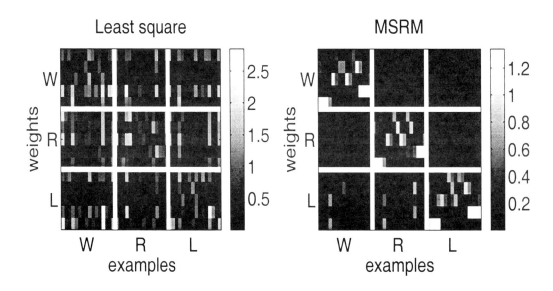

78

7 Conclusions and outlook

In this article we have presented first results that explore the idea of a linear combination of prototypical motion sequences for the synthesis and analysis of video sequences. We are presently trying to generalize the same techniques for an application to real video sequences.

Our results seem to be promising for analysis and synthesis. For synthesis it has has to be explored if interpolated sequences with sufficiently high quality can be obtained, for instance by a separate linear combination of texture (brightness) and shape (spatial shifts) [1]. For recognition, potentially higher distortions of the interpolated patterns can be tolerated. Instead of using specific object points as features we are planning to apply optic flow algorithms to real image data (cf. also [14, 1]). Using characteristic key points to simplify the correspondence process may however be helpful in graphics animation applications of our method.

The proposed method for the integration of a priori knowledge in the estimation of the linear weights seems to be an interesting extension of the structural risk minimization principle. Most applications so far, have mainly focused on minimizing the VC dimension of the approximating function set, but did not include problem-specific a priori knowledge about the structure of the admissible function set. The quadratic programming procedure sets irrelevant coefficients, and coefficients that do not fulfill the constraints to zero. This should lead to a high robustness of the described method, in comparison with alternative procedures that are based on weighted least squares estimation.

Acknowledgments

This work was supported by the Deutsche Forschungsgemeinschaft.

Appendix A: Details of the correspondence algorithm

The real implementation deals with image sequences that are sampled equally-spaced in time with sampling time T, indicated in the following by $\mathbf{x}_i[n]$. The algorithm that we used was inspired dynamic time warping methods in speech recognition [8]. (For an application of similar techniques to the time warping of gestures see [2].) Compared to such algorithms, our method tries to minimize the computational effort by minimizing the number of sampled image frames, and by warping between the sampling images. In this way we can emulate a time continuous sequence of images.

Our correspondence algorithm consists of two steps. The first step is based on a dynamic programming algorithm for path optimization. Given the N frames of the two image sequences $\mathbf{x}_1$ and $\mathbf{x}_2$, that have to be brought into correspondence, we calculate for each frame pairing with discrete times n and n', $1 \leq n, n' \leq N$, the error function value:

$$E_d(n, n') = |\mathbf{x}_1[n] - \mathbf{x}_2[n']|^2 + \lambda(n - n')^2 \, T^2 \qquad (14)$$

The dynamic programming algorithm tries to find a path in the n-n'-plane with minimum cost, where the cost is the sum values of the function E_d along the path. The algorithm starts with the index pair $n = 1$ and $n' = 1$. Along the path n always increases by one. To implement the monotonicity constraint (5), the set of permitted path transitions for n' is restricted. If we indicate by $n'[n]$ the value of the index n' that is associated with the index n, the possible values of $n'[n]$ are restricted through the inequality:

$$n'[n - 1] \leq n'[n] \leq n'[n - 1] + 2 \qquad (15)$$

To enforce the end-point constraints (6) we introduced the additional restrictions:

$$2n - N \leq n'[n] \leq N \qquad (16)$$

The second step of our algorithm determines the exact spatial and temporal shifts by linearly interpolating between the discrete frames of the sequence $\mathbf{x}_1$. For this purpose we construct a time-continuous sequence by warping linearly between the frames of the time discrete sequence. The interpolated (quasi) time-continuous image sequence in the time intervals $I_1 = [(n - 1)T, nT]$ and $I_2 = [nT, (n + 1)T]$ is given by the equation:

$$\mathbf{x}_1(t) = \begin{cases} \mathbf{x}_1[n] - (n - t/T) \, \mathbf{d}_1[n - 1] & \text{for } t \in I_1 \\ \mathbf{x}_1[n] + (n - t/T) \, \mathbf{d}_1[n] & \text{for } t \in I_2 \end{cases} \qquad (17)$$

with

$$\mathbf{d}_1[n] = \mathbf{x}_1[n + 1] - \mathbf{x}_1[n]. \qquad (18)$$

Introducing this this approximation into the error function (4), one can analytically calculate the optimal time shifts within the two time intervals. (The integral was replaced by a sum over the discrete time events that are indexed by n.) resulting in the expression

$$\tau(nT) = T \left(\frac{n|\mathbf{d}_1|^2 + \lambda T^2 n' \pm \mathbf{d}'_{21}[n', n] \, \mathbf{d}_1}{\lambda T^2 + |\mathbf{d}_1|^2} - n' \right) \qquad (19)$$

where the vector $\mathbf{d}_{21}$ is given by

$$\mathbf{d}_{21} = \mathbf{x}_2[n'] - \mathbf{x}_1[n].$$

In the interval I_1 the first sign has to be chosen, and $\mathbf{d}_1 = \mathbf{d}_1[n - 1]$, whereas for the interval I_2 the second sign is valid and $\mathbf{d}_1 = \mathbf{d}_1[n]$. In this way two candidate values for the time shift $\tau(nT)$ are obtained, one for each interpolation interval. We selected the value that led to a smaller value of the error function E_c. Given the calculated optimal time shifts, one can use equation (17) to obtain the associated optimal spatial shifts.

Appendix B: Quadratic programming problem for the MSRM

By introducing the new non-negative variable vectors $\mathbf{z}$ and $\mathbf{z}^*$ one can rewrite the error function in (13) in the form:

$$\tilde{E}_m(\mathbf{z}, \mathbf{z}^*) = [\mathbf{z}'\ \mathbf{z}^{*\prime}]\, \mathbf{W}_m \begin{bmatrix} \mathbf{z} \\ \mathbf{z}^* \end{bmatrix} + C\,|\boldsymbol{\zeta}|^2 \qquad (20)$$

where the symmetric matrix $\mathbf{W}_m$ is given by

$$\mathbf{W}_m = \begin{bmatrix} \mathbf{W} & \mathbf{W}_0 \\ \mathbf{W}_0 & \mathbf{W} \end{bmatrix} \qquad (21)$$

and where $\mathbf{W}_0$ by setting the diagonal elements of $\mathbf{W}$ to zero. (This procedure is important to obtain a non-degenerate quadratic term, since otherwise the matrix has rank zero.)

The constraints have to be reformulated in the form:

$$[\mathbf{K}, -\mathbf{K}] \begin{bmatrix} \mathbf{z} \\ \mathbf{z}^* \end{bmatrix} = \mathbf{a} + \boldsymbol{\zeta} \qquad (22)$$

$$\mathbf{z} \geq \mathbf{0} \qquad (23)$$

$$\mathbf{z}^* \geq \mathbf{0} \qquad (24)$$

This is a standard quadratic programming problem with a number of equality and inequality constraints for which efficient solution algorithms exist [6]. The quadratic programming algorithm was part of the MATLAB optimization toolbox. We removed redundant (almost) linear dependent equations from the constraint system $\mathbf{Kc} = \mathbf{a}$ to ensure a fast convergence of the algorithm.

References

[1] D. Beymer and T. Poggio. Image representations for visual learning. *Science*, 272:1905–1909, 1996.

[2] T. J. Darrell, I. A. Essa, and A. Pentland. Task-specific gesture analysis in real-time using interpolated views. Technical Report 364, Massachusetts Institute of Technology, Cambridge, MA, 1995.

[3] J. W. Davis and A. F. Bobick. The representation and recognition of action using temporal templates. Technical Report 402, Massachusetts Institute of Technology, Cambridge, MA, 1996.

[4] I. A. Essa and A. P. Pentland. Coding, analysis, interpretation and recognition of facial expressions. *IEEE Transactions on Pattern Recognition and Machine Intelligence*, 19:(in press), 1997.

[5] T. Ezzat and T. Poggio. Miketalk: A talking facial display based on morphing visemes. In *Proceedings of the Computer Animation Conference, Philadelphia, PA*, 1998.

[6] P. E. Gill, W. Murray, and M. H. Wright. *Mathematical optimization*. Academic Press, London, 1981.

[7] M. J. Jones. *Multidimensional morphable models: A framework for representing and matching object classes*. PhD thesis, Dept. of Computer Science, Cambridge, MA, 1997.

[8] B. H. Juang and L. R. Rabiner. *Fundamentals of Speech Recognition*. Prentic-Hall, Englewood Cliffs,n NJ, 1993.

[9] S. A. Niyogi and E. H. Adelson. Analyzing and recognizing walking figures in XYT. Technical Report 223, Massachusetts Institute of Technology, Cambridge, MA, 1994.

[10] J. O'Rourke and N. I. Badler. Model-based analysis of human motion using constraint propagation. *IEEE Transactions on Pattern Recognition and Machine Intelligence*, 2:522–536, 1982.

[11] T. Poggio and S. Edelman. A network that learns to recognize three-dimensional objects. *Nature*, 343:263–266, 1990.

[12] V. N. Vapnik. *Statistical Learning Theory*. Wiley, New York, 1998.

[13] T. Vetter. Synthesis of novel views from a single face image. *International Journal of Computer Vision*, 28(2):103–116, 1998.

[14] T. Vetter and T. Poggio. Linear object classes and image synthesis from a single example. *IEEE Transactions on Pattern Recognition and Machine Intelligence*, 19(7):733–742, 1997.

[15] Y. Yacoob and M. J. Black. Parameertized modeling and recognition of activities. *Computer vision and Image Understanding*, (in press), 1999.

Real-time Rendering System of Moving Objects

Yutaka Kunita   Masahiko Inami   Taro Maeda   Susumu Tachi

Department of Mathematical Engineering and Information Physics
Graduate Shool of Engineering, The University of Tokyo
7-3-1 Hongo, Bunkyo-ku, Tokyo 113-8656, Japan
{kuni, minami, maeda, tachi}@star.t.u-tokyo.ac.jp

Abstract

We have been developing a system named "mutual tele-existence" which allows for face-to-face communication between remote users [14]. Although image-based rendering (IBR) is suitable for rendering human figures with a complex geometry, conventional IBR techniques cannot readily be applied to our system. Because most IBR techniques include time-consuming processes, they cannot capture the source images and simultaneously render the destination images. In this paper, we propose a novel method focusing on real-time rendering. Moreover, we introduce equivalent depth of field to measure the fidelity of the synthesized image. If the object is in this range, accurate rendering is guaranteed. Then, we introduce a prototype machine that has 12 synchronized cameras on the linear actuator. Finally, we present some experimental results of our prototype machine.

1 Introduction

We have been developing a system which allows for face-to-face communication between remote users[14]. In this system, users who are far apart in the real world share computer-generated three-dimensional space. Figure 1 shows the concept behind our system. In this system, users communicate with one another by each entering a booth which has a cylindrical structure surrounding the user. This structure works both as the display device and the

image-capturing device. It displays stereoscopic images of the computer-generated three-dimensional space around the user just like CAVE[3], and simultaneously captures a set of images from all sides of the user.

Figure 1: The concept of our tele-communication system.

In most conventional tele-conferencing systems, users exchange images from a fixed viewpoint only. However, we believe that our system should display the images from the users' eye position in the computer-generated three-dimensional space, in order to provide the users with the feeling that they are all in the same place, i.e. "presence."

However, the set of images captured by the booth is the one from the fixed orbit around the booth, and the images to be displayed are the ones from the

81

users' viewpoints in the computer-generated space. Therefore, generating images from arbitrary viewpoints using a set of images from the fixed orbit would be a technological key to realizing our system.

A considerable amount of research is available about this kind of rendering technique [2], [4], [5], [6], [7], [8], [9], [10], [11], [12], [13]; however, all these studies present the same problem in their application to tele-conferencing systems, namely, that take too much time.

For example, some techniques take the approach of making use of geometric information [6],[10],[11],[12]. One typical piece of geometric information is a "depth map," the depth values which corresponds to each pixel of the image. Once the depth map is acquired, it is easy to synthesize the images from arbitrary viewpoints. However, the process of acquiring this depth map is very time-consuming and lacks robustness.

In another approach, geometric information is not used. Instead, a subset of the "plenoptic function"[1] as a representation of the data stage is used[5],[8]. The plenoptic function is a 5-dimensional function which describes the ray's intensity in all positions and at all angles. If the plenoptic function could be acquired, it would also be possible to acquire images from arbitrary viewpoints. However, this is actually impossible. So, the dimension of the prenoptic function is usually reduced from 5 to 4 by assuming a free space and transparency of the route of the ray. But, since the amount of data of this 4-dimensional function is still too large, it is acquired in an off-line process. The technique using the representation of EPI (epipolar-plane images) [7] can also be categorized here.

To overcome the difficulties outlined above, we here propose a novel method focusing on real-time rendering of moving objects in the real world. This method has the following features:

1. Only one parameter of the object's distance is needed. Thus, geometric information such as a "depth map" is not required.

2. Fast rendering is possible by making use of graphic hardware acceleration of texture mapping.

3. The data processed by the rendering computer are reduced in advance at the stage of capturing the source images.

This paper is organized as follows.

In Section2, we describe the basic theory of our rendering method. Although our method does not need explicit geometric information (Feature 1), the distance of one typical point of the object is required. This is analogous to the way in which we take photos with a single camera: we adjust the focal distance to one point of the object. In this analogy, we define "equivalent focal distance" and "equivalent depth of field," which represent the supposed distance from cameras to objects and the range of distance within which objects are guaranteed correct image synthesis, respectively. Fast-rendering algorithms are also included using texture-mapping (Feature 2) in this section.

In Section 3, we introduce our prototype machine, which has 12 synchronized cameras. These cameras, which are located in a row on the linear actuator, will in future acquire images during a reciprocating motion. However, the cameras are still at present. In this prototype system, the rendering machine does not capture the image signals from all 12 cameras but only the one signal that has to be rendered at the time. Because of this, this system uses only one video-capture device, and the amount of image data required to deal with it is extremely reduced (Feature 3).

Next, in Section 4, we show some experimental results using this prototype system. We succeed in real-time rendering of moving objects in the real world.

Finally, in Section 5, we present our conclusions and project out future work.

2 Image Synthesis Method

2.1 Plenoptic Function

The plenoptic function[1] is a 5-dimensional function which describes the ray's intensity in all positions and at all angles. If the plenoptic function could be achieved, images from arbitrary viewpoints could also be obtained. Since this is actually impossible in the real world, there is an approach which reduces the dimension of the plenoptic function from 5 to 4 by assuming a free space and the transparency of the ray's route [5],[8]. Although this 4-dimensional function is easier to achieve than the plenoptic function, the amount of data is still considerably large. Moreover, the rendering method using such a function requires the ray to have relatively high-sampling density. Because of these characteristics, the ray-sampling process of this kind of technique is very time-consuming. Thus, the objects are assumed to be static. In the following subsection, we describe the method we employed for our real-time rendering system. Although this method is based on the concept of the plenoptic function, the required sampling densities are relatively low and the rendering process is extremely simple.

2.2 Basic Theory

Hereafter, we explain our theory in the two-dimensional space for the sake of simplicity. However, it can be easily extended to the three-dimensional space without loss of generality.

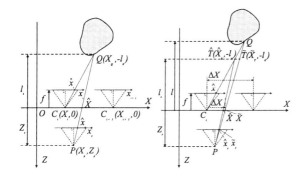

Figure 2: **Left**: Image synthesis at the viewposition P using a set of cameras C_i which are aligned on the X-axis. **Right**: Error between the desired position $\tilde{x_P}$ and the synthesized position $\hat{x_P}$ of Q on the image plane, when Q is not at the equivalent focal distance l_0.

In The left of Figure 2, plural cameras (focal length: f) are aligned so that their centers of projection $C_i(X_i, 0)$ are located on the X-axis. These cameras capture the images of the object in region $Z < 0$. Each camera has an image plane at length f from the center of projection C_i, which has a coordinate x_i. Let $P(X_P, Z_P)$ denote the virtual camera's viewpoint ($Z_P > 0$) and suppose this virtual camera also has an image plane: x_P. Our purpose is to describe the method used for synthesizing the image from P: $g_P(x_P)$ using a set of images of camera C_i: $g_i(x_i)$.

The ray which makes the image where $x_P = \hat{x_P}$ intersects the X-axis at point $X = \hat{X}$. If there were a camera at point $\hat{X}$, the image of the ray sampled by the camera would be the same as that of P, assuming there is no occluder (free space) and the route has transparency. However, a case in which there is no camera at point $\hat{X}$ could happen at low sampling densities, i.e. when the intervals of the cameras are long.

However, the ray which makes the image at $x_P = \hat{x_P}$ comes from $Q(X_Q, -l_0)$, and the ray which makes the image at $x_i = \hat{x_i}$ comes from the same point as well. Assuming that the surface of the object is diffusive, it can be said that

$$g_P(x_P) = g_i(x_i) \qquad (1)$$

where the following equation is established between $\hat{x}_p$, $\hat{x}_i$.

$$X_i + l_0 \cdot \frac{\hat{x_i}}{f} = X_P + (l_0 + Z_P) \cdot \frac{\hat{x_P}}{f} = X_Q \qquad (2)$$

In the equation above, l_0 is an approximate distance to the object, which we call "equivalent focal distance." Note that this value is not an array of distances like a depth map but, rather, a length to a representative point of the object's surface, exactly like a camera's focal distance.

Of course, not every point on the surface of the object exists at all times on length l_0, except for objects which have a planer surface $Z = -l_0$. In such cases, the image of Q is synthesized at the wrong position by the method mentioned above.

For example, in the right of Figure 2, the ray from Q makes the image at $x_i = \hat{x_i}$ of camera C_i. However, using the equivalent focal distance l_0, which differs from l (the correct distance to Q), the image of Q is synthesized at position $\hat{x_p}$, whereas the image of Q should be synthesized at position $\tilde{x_P}$. Now, we define the error of the positions between the synthesized image and the correct image as:

$$\Delta x_P \equiv \hat{x_P} - \tilde{x_P} \qquad (3)$$

Then, the following equations are established providing $(\tilde{X}_t, -l_0)$ denotes the point of intersection of $Z = -l_0$ and PQ, and $(\hat{X}_t, -l_0)$ that of $Z = -l_0$ and C_i, respectively.

$$\Delta x_P = \frac{f}{l_0 + z_P}(\hat{X}_t - \tilde{X}_t) \qquad (4)$$

$$\hat{X}_t - \tilde{X}_t = \frac{l - l_0}{l}(X_i - \tilde{X}) \qquad (5)$$

By substituting Equation(5) into Equation(4), we obtain

$$\Delta x_P = \frac{l - l_0}{l} \cdot \frac{f}{l_0 + z_P} \cdot (X_i - \tilde{X}) \qquad (6)$$

Besides,

$$\begin{aligned} X_i - \tilde{X} &= (\hat{X} - \tilde{X}) + (X_i - \hat{X}) \\ &= \frac{z_P}{f} \cdot \Delta x_P + (X_i - \hat{X}) \end{aligned} \qquad (7)$$

Finally, by substituting equation (7) into equation (6), we obtain the following equation:

$$\Delta x_P = \frac{f(l - l_0)}{l_0(1 + Z_P)} \cdot (\hat{X} - X_i) \qquad (8)$$

2.3 Equivalent Depth of Field

Now, let δ denote the maximum error allowed. After this, we determine the range of l, where $|\Delta x_P| \leq \delta$ for all $\hat{X}$.

As we can see in Equation(8), the absolute error of the image position $|\Delta x_P|$ is in proportion to $|\hat{X} - X_i|$. Therefore, we choose camera C_i among several cameras so that $|\hat{X} - X_i|$ gets the minimum value. When the cameras are aligned at the intervals ΔX, we must choose camera C_i so that $|\hat{X} - X_i| \leq \frac{\Delta X}{2}$. Hence, from Equation(8) it can be said that

$$|\Delta x_P| \leq \frac{f|l - l_0|}{l_0(1 + Z_P)} \cdot \frac{\Delta X}{2} \qquad (9)$$

By solving (*the right side of Equation(9)* $= \delta$) for l, we obtain two solutions $l = l_1, l_2 (l_1 \leq l_0 \leq l_2)$, as follows:

$$l_1 = l_0 \cdot \frac{1}{1 + \frac{l_0 + Z_P}{\frac{f}{\delta}\frac{\Delta X}{2} + Z_P}} \qquad (10)$$

$$l_2 = l_0 \cdot \frac{1}{1 - \frac{l_0 + Z_P}{\frac{f}{\delta}\frac{\Delta X}{2} + Z_P}} \qquad (11)$$

Then, $|\Delta x_P| \leq \delta$ is established for all l which satisfies $l_1 \leq l \leq l_2$.

If we let δ be the length of one pixel on the image plane, the points on the objects at the distance within $l_1 \leq l \leq l_2$ are guaranteed to be synthesized at actually correct positions whose errors are within one pixel. We call this range of distance $\Delta l \equiv l_2 - l_1$ the "*equivalent depth of field.*" Δl is a function of ΔX and monotone decreasing.

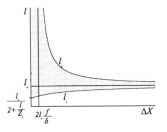

Figure 3: The graph of the equivalent depth of field. The equivalent depth of field is expressed by the length between l_1 and l_2.

Figure 3 shows a graph plotting l_1 and l_2 versus ΔX. In this figure, the equivalent depth of field is expressed by the length between l_1 and l_2. Note that $l_1 = \infty$ when $\Delta X = 2l_0 \cdot \frac{\delta}{f}$. If we place the cameras at smaller intervals than $2l_0 \cdot \frac{\delta}{f}$, all the points on the objects at length $l \geq l_1$ can be correctly synthesized.

2.4 Rendering Algorithm

In this subsection, we will describe two different algorithms which implement the method mentioned above.

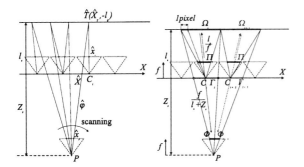

Figure 4: **Left**:Rendering by ray-tracing algorithm. **Right**:Rendering by multi-texture-mapping algorithm.

2.4.1 Ray-Tracing Algorithm

In this algorithm, the image is acquired from the virtual viewpoint P by scanning the rays which intersect P. See the left of Figure4.

The whole process is as follows:

For each $x_P = \hat{x_P}$,

1. Let $\hat{\varphi}$ denote the ray which makes the image at $x_P = \hat{x_P}$; $\hat{\varphi}$ intersects $Z = 0, -l_0$ at $X = \hat{X}, \hat{X_T}$ respectively, where $\hat{X} = X_P + Z_P \frac{x_P}{f}$ and $\hat{X_T} = X_P + (Z_P + l_0)\frac{x_P}{f}$.

2. Choose camera C_i, whose $X-$coordinate X_i is nearest to $\hat{X}$.

3. Obtain $\hat{x_i}$, which is the intersection of the line from $(\hat{X_T}, -l_0)$ to C_i and the image plane of the camera C_i. This process corresponds with solving Equation(2) for $\hat{x_i}$.

4. Copy the image of camera C_i at $x_i = \hat{x_i}$ to that of the virtual viewpoint P at $x_P = \hat{x_P}$, that is to say: $g_P(\hat{x_P}) = g_i(\hat{x_i})$.

The algorithm mentioned above includes many repetitions, and the calculation processes which find $\hat{x_Q}$ corresponding to $\hat{x_P}$ are rather complicated. Therefore, this algorithm is not suitable for real-time rendering

2.4.2 Multi-texture Mapping Method

Unlike the algorithm explained above, the one below is very straightforward and designed for real-time rendering.

See the right of Figure 4. First, we define Γ_i which is the region on $Z = 0$ as:

$$\Gamma_i \equiv \left(\frac{X_{i-1} + X_i}{2}, \frac{X_i + X_{i+1}}{2} \right]. \qquad (12)$$

Suppose the rays go through P, whose X-intercepts are within Γ_i i.e., $\hat{X} \in \Gamma_i$. The closest camera to these intercepts is surely C_i. If the images from P corresponding to these rays were rendered with the previous ray-tracing method, the source images within Π_i would be copied to the destination images within Φ_i. Besides, the rays would intersect $Z = -l_0$ within the region Ω_i. From a simple similarity, we can obtain:

$$\text{len}\,\Omega_i = \frac{l_0}{f} \cdot \text{len}\,\Pi_i \qquad (13)$$

$$\text{len}\,\Phi_i = \frac{f}{l_0 + Z_P} \cdot \text{len}\,\Omega_i \qquad (14)$$

where "len" expresses the length of the region. From Equation(13)(14),

$$\text{len}\,\Phi_i = \frac{l_0}{l_0 + Z_P} \cdot \text{len}\,\Pi_i \qquad (15)$$

Because the correspondence between $\hat{x_P} \in \Phi_i$ and $\hat{x_i} \in \Pi_i$ is linear, we can copy the source image $g_i(x_i \in \Pi)$ to the destination image $g_P(x_P \in \Phi_i)$ with the scaling ratio $l_0/(l_0 + Z_P)$ all at once. By performing such a procedure for each i, we can obtain the desired image from a virtual viewpoint P without scanning each ray through P.

Furthermore, this scaling procedure can be done automatically with a general 3-D graphic library as follows:

1. Construct a scene consisting of a viewpoint P and a plane T.

2. For each i, paste the corresponding image of camera C_i: $g_i(x_i \in \Pi_i)$ to region Ω_i on plane T as a texture-mapping image. By taking the

ratio [1 pixel of Π_i]: [1 pixel of Ω_i] as [len Π_i]: [len Ω_i] $(= f : l_0)$, this process is equal to simple memory copy without scaling from the image captured by the camera to the texture-mapping image.

3. Render the perspective image from P.

Note that none of the processes above includes explicit scaling procedures, but we can obtain the same effect. Each image of camera C_i: $g_i(x_i \in \Pi_i)$ is copied to Ω_i on plane T at scaling ratio l_0/f. Then, these images of region Ω_i are rendered in the image plane of P at scaling ratio $f/(l_0 + Z_P)$. Thus, each $g_i(x_i \in \Pi_i)$ is rendered on the image plane of P at scaling ratio $l_0/(l_0 + Z_P)$ as a result.

This rendering algorithm combines simplicity and speed by making use of hardware acceleration in texture mapping such as scaling and smoothing. By employing this method, our prototype system, which we describe in the next section, realized real-time rendering.

3 Prototype System

3.1 Overall

The left picture of Figure 5 shows our prototype system, and that on the right is its block diagram. This system consists of a camera unit, a rendering PC, and a control PC.

In the camera unit, 12 small color CCD cameras (Toshiba IK-C40, the length of one pixel $\delta \sim 0.01mm$) are aligned horizontally in a row on the linear actuator at intervals of 54mm. Very wide-angle lens (focal distance $f = 3.5mm$) are attached to the cameras. In future, the actuator will reciprocate while the cameras acquire the image. At present, the actuator remains still. These cameras are located on the gantry with rotating 90° around their optical axes. Thus, the direction of their scanning lines is vertical. Moreover, all these cameras are synchronized by the same genlock signal.

The rendering PC continuously captures a video signal from the camera unit by one video-capturing board. Note that if we intended to capture all 12 video signals, 12 video-capturing boards would be required, which would not be practical. Consequently, we installed a video switch between the camera unit and the rendering PC, allowing only one scanning line among 12 scanning lines to be selectively captured by one video-capturing board. The timing of switching channels is synchronized with the cameras' genlock signal.

The control PC indicates the channel of this switch and controls the motion of the linear actuator. This control PC and the rendering PC exchange data fast by using a shared memory.

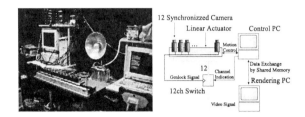

Figure 5: **Left**:the overview of our prototype system. **Right**:the block diagram of our prototype system.

3.2 Implementation of Rendering

In this subsection, we describe the implementation of real-time rendering of our prototype system. We employ the multi-texture-mapping algorithm mentioned in the previous section.

First, with a virtual viewpoint given by a user, the rendering PC calcurates the regions of each camera's image that are used for multi-texture-mapping. Because the cameras are aligned horizontally, each region is made by dividing the whole image of the camera horizonally. Thus, its shape is a vertically long column.

Next, the information of the region is send to the control PC and used as an indication of the video switch. The timing of switching is synchronous with the camerass' scanning, and the direction of the cameras' scanning line is vertical. In this way, the rendering PC can selectively capture the necessary column image from the cameras.

Then, the captured images are texture-mapped on a plane at the distance of the equivalent focal distance in the virtual three-dimensional space. This process is equal to the simple memory copy mentioned previously.

Finally, the rendering PC renders the scene by using a 3D graphic library.

One cycle of all these processes is finished within video rate ($1/30[sec]$), so we can say our system realizes real-time rendering.

Some conventional IBR systems capture all the images from the cameras and construct bulky data as a subset of the plenoptic funcion, whereas our system reduces the image data to deal with before capturing them at the analog signal level. On the other hand, the scaling process is rapidly carried out by digital graphic hardware. This combination of analog and digital technologies is the key to real-time rendering.

4 Experimental Result

4.1 Relation between Sampling Density and Equivalent Depth of Field

In this experiment, we synthesize the images of a static object with with different camera intervals ΔX.

The upper left of Figure 6 shows the positions of the cameras, the virtual viewpoint, and the two objects. The cameras are aligned on $Z = 0$. The virtual viewpoint is at $Z = 50[mm]$. The two objects are on $Z = -350$ and $-70[mm]$, respectively.

The upper right shows a graph plotting the equivalent depth of field on condition that the cameras' parameters $f = 3.5[mm]$, $\delta = 0.01[mm]$, and the equivalent focal distance $l_0 = 350[mm]$, i.e., focused on the front object.

When $\Delta X = 4[mm]$, the equivalent depth of field is $522[mm]$ and the lower left picture is synthesized. As we can see, both the image of the back object and that of the front object are synthesized accurately.

On the other hand, when $\Delta X = 30[mm]$, the equivalent depth of field is $53mm$, which is not long enough to synthesize the image of the back object.

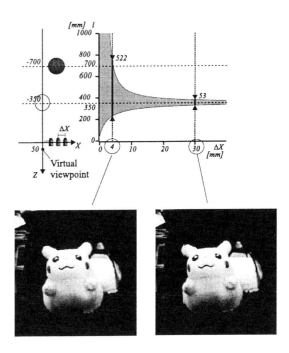

Figure 6: Image synthesis of static objects with different camera intervals ΔX.

The lower right picture shows the discontinuity on the back object.

4.2 Correct Expression of Occlusion

In this experiment, we compare the multi-texture mapping algorithm introduced previously with conventional texture mapping using an image from a single camera.

The upper part of Figure 7 shows a scene, where the cameras are aligned on $Z = 0$ with intervals of $54mm$, the moving object is near $(0, -1000)$, and the virtual viewpoint P is at $(200, 500)$. The object shades his face with his hand against the virtual viewpoint P. Therefore, the object's face should not be seen from P.

The lower left of Figure 7 shows the image synthesized by texture-mapping the image in camera C_0 on plane $T(Z = -1000)$. We can see the object's face, and the correct occlusion is not expressed. On the Contraty, the lower right image which is synthesized

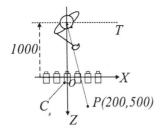

Figure 7: Comparison between the images synthesized by using a single texture (left) and multiple textures (right). While the one on the left can not express correct occlusion, the one on the right can.

by the multi-texture mapping method, succeeds in expressing the correct occlusion.

5 Conclusions

We introduced a novel image synthesis method for our tele-communication system focusing on real-time rendering. Next, we mentioned "*equivalent depth of field*" to measure the fidelity of the synthesized images. Then, we showed a prototype machine which realized real-time rendering and its results. A topic of future work will be to synthesize images during reciprocating cameras on a linear actuator. By moving cameras, our prototype system can synthesize images at higher spatial sampling densities. Then, extending an image synthesis method proposed in this paper, we will investigte a method where cameras are arranged around the object.

References

[1] E. H. Adelson and J. R. Bergen. *The Plenoptic Function and the Elements of Early Vision*, chapter 1. The MIT Press, 1991.

[2] S. E. Chen and L. Williams. View interpolation for image synthesis. In *SIGGRAPH'93 Conference Proceedings*, pages 279–288, 1993.

[3] C. Cruz-Neira, D. J. Sandin, and T. A. De-Fanti. Surround-screen projection-based virtual reality: The design and imprementation of the cave. In *SIGGRAPH'93 Conference Proceedings*, pages 135–142, 1993.

[4] P. E. Debevec, C. J. Taylor, and J. Malik. Modeling and rendering architecture from photographs: A hybrid geomtry- and image-based approach. In *SIGGRAPH'96 Conference Proceedings*, pages 11–20, 1996.

[5] S. J. Gortler, R. Grzeszczuk, R. Szeliski, and M. F. Cohen. The lumigraph. In *SIGGRAPH'96 Conference Proceedings*, pages 43–54, 1996.

[6] T. Kanade, P. J. Narayanan, and P. Rander. Virtualized reality: Being mobile in a visual scene. In *Proceedings of the 5th International Conference on Artificial Reality and Tele-Existence (ICAT 95)*, pages 133–142, 1995.

[7] A. Katayama, K. Tanaka, T. Oshino, and H. Tamura. A viewpoint dependent stereoscopic display using interpolation of multi-viewpoint images. In *Stereoscopic Displays and Virtual Reality Systems II*, volume 2409, pages 11–20. SPIE, 1995.

[8] M. Levoy and P. Hanrahan. Light field rendering. In *SIGGRAPH'96 Conference Proceedings*, pages 31–41, 1996.

[9] L. McMillan and G. Bishop. Plenoptic modeling: An image-based rendering system. In *SIGGRAPH'95 Conference Proceedings*, pages 39–46, 1995.

[10] S. Moezzi, A. Katkere, D. Y. Kuramura, and R. Jain. Immersive video. In *Proceedings of VRAIS '96*, pages 17–24. IEEE, 1996.

[11] P. Rademacher and G. Bishop. Multiple-center-of-projection images. In *SIGGRAPH'98 Conference Proceedings*, pages 199–206, 1998.

[12] R. Raskar, G. Welch, M. Cutts, A. Lake, L. Stesin, and H. Fuchs. The office of the future: A unified approach to image-based modeling and spatially immersive displays. In *SIGGRAPH'98 Conference Proceedings*, pages 179–188, 1998.

[13] J. Shade, S. Gortler, L. wei He, and R. Szeliski. Layered depth images. In *SIGGRAPH'98 Conference Proceedings*, pages 231–242, 1998.

[14] S. Tachi, T. Maeda, Y. Yanagida, M. Koyanagi, and H. Yokoyama. A method of mutual tele-existence in a virtual environment. In *Proceedings of the 6th International Conference on Artificial Reality and Tele-Existence (ICAT 96)*, pages 9–18, 1996.

Author Index

— *Notes* —

— *Notes* —

IEEE

COMPUTER
SOCIETY

Press Activities Board

IEEE Computer Society Publications

The world-renowned IEEE Computer Society publishes, promotes, and distributes a wide variety of authoritative computer science and engineering texts. These books are available from most retail outlets. Visit the Online Catalog, *http://computer.org*, for a list of products.

IEEE Computer Society Proceedings

The IEEE Computer Society also produces and actively promotes the proceedings of more than 141 acclaimed international conferences each year in multimedia formats that include hard and softcover books, CD-ROMs, videos, and on-line publications.

For information on the IEEE Computer Society proceedings, send e-mail to cs.books@computer.org or write to Proceedings, IEEE Computer Society, P.O. Box 3014, 10662 Los Vaqueros Circle, Los Alamitos, CA 90720-1314. Telephone +1 714-821-8380. FAX +1 714-761-1784.

Additional information regarding the Computer Society, conferences and proceedings, CD-ROMs, videos, and books can also be accessed from our web site at *http://computer.org/cspress*